HEINRICH HEINE

BOOKS BY MICHAEL MONAHAN

―――――

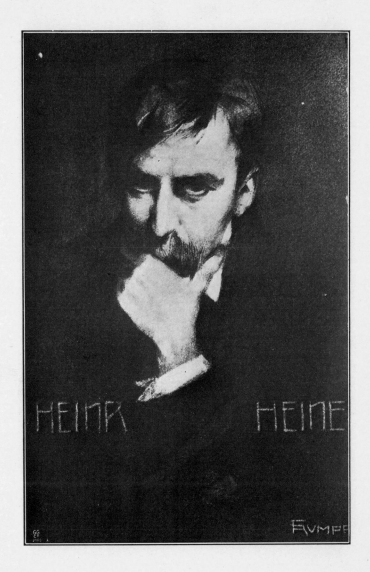

HEINRICH HEINE

ROMANCE AND TRAGEDY
OF THE POET'S LIFE

With a Critical Appreciation

By

MICHAEL MONAHAN

NICHOLAS L. BROWN
NEW YORK   1924

To
Rudolph Jay Schaefer

Two old friends and a flask of Moselle,
The *Buch der Lieder*—and all is well!

Two old friends with a genial thought,
And a ripened lore that the years have brought.

Black were their heads when they cronied first,
But for wine and song are they still athirst.

Time the deceiver his tale has told,
Palmed on them silver in lieu of gold.

Ho! ho! they laugh at the roguish turn;
With snow at the top their hearts still burn.

Softly, ay softly, year adds to year,
As the Rhenish glows in the crystal clear.

And the grape blooms aye on the banks of Rhine,
While they cheer their journey with song and
    wine.

Yes, the grape by the Rhine still blooms alway,
And the Poet lures in his deathless lay.

M. M.

New York
    July, 1923

5

THE CONTENTS

THE CONTENTS

PART III

ART AND PERSONALITY

ILLUSTRATION

FOREWORD

THE poet Heine's fame, which has been as a sword of conflict thrown into the world, especially in his German Fatherland, is giving proof of its intense vitality in the discussions following upon the Great War. No name is oftener cited than his, no writings are more eagerly scanned for confirmation of the past or light upon the troubled future than those of the great rebel-poet. Many pens are recalling his life-long devotion to the cause of liberty; his heroic and passionate crusade against old tyrannies and rooted abuses of privilege and caste in his native Germany, together with his championship of the oppressed in every land which moved Matthew Arnold to name him "a Paladin of the modern spirit"; his long exile in France and the interdiction of his books through many years by the Prussian Government; finally, his political vision and power of reading the future, which has been in several instances extraordinarily verified (*e. g.,* his forecast of the Franco-German

9

War of 1870-71, and his prediction of the growth
of Socialism throughout Europe). One may
turn to these words of Heine uttered many years
ago, and feel that in the light of recent tremen-
dous events they are instinct with prophecy:

"There are no nations in Europe now; there
are only two factions. One is called ARISTOC-
RACY: it thinks itself privileged by birth and
monopolizes all the glories of the commonalty.
The other faction is called DEMOCRACY: it vin-
dicates the rights of MAN, and in the name of
Reason demands the abolition of the privileges
of birth."

It is recalled that Heine was both a Leader
and a Prophet of the great democratic movement, which has advanced by painfully slow yet
certain strides since his death, and which but
yesterday underwent its great trial by fire on the
battlefields of Europe. Liberty had no bolder
tribune than he nor one more feared and hated
by the upholders of ancient privilege and des-
potism. He was not a patriot in the narrow
sense: much as he loved Germany, much as he
had suffered for the cause of German liberties,
he demanded freedom for the whole world—
the emancipation of all oppressed peoples!
Seventy-five years ago he declared that Europe

was old enough to be its own master, and that it was breaking away from the iron leading-strings still held by the privileged aristocracy. His prophetic ken probed even farther than this, for he predicted the emancipation of kings!—which event will perhaps be determined in our time.

The invocation, then, of this "brave soldier of the liberation-war of humanity" (as he not unworthily called himself) in any discussion of the World War or its present issues, can only be regarded as a natural tribute to the man who as poet and propagandist aided powerfully in continuing the impulse of the French Revolution. And we see also that he spoke not vainly when he claimed his reward and recognition from the future.

However, this by the way, and the sagacious reader need not fear that I am trying to palm off on him a belated war-book in the guise of *belles-lettres*. I hasten to assure him that my book is conceived throughout in the literary spirit, and written without conscious reference to the burning questions of the hour. Further, it is the result of a life-long reading of the Poet and of no small part of the literature that has gathered about his name and fame.

To make an end: this little work is a tribute

of love and admiration to a writer who has possessed me from my youth up, with whom I have had some of the best hours that can fall to a reading man, and of whose charm I am still unwearied. A writer whose greatness and universal appeal lift him beyond the bounds of race and creed, the geographic limits of the patriot and the systems of the political doctrinaire; who belongs in fact to that phalanx of men of genius, warriors of thought, whose mere names are the rallying points of humanity.

MICHAEL MONAHAN

New York
October, 1923

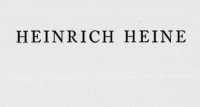

HEINRICH HEINE

PART I

THE MARBLE VENUS

THE nightingale, she sweetly sang,
I could withstand no longer;
And when I kissed her lovely face,
I knew which was the stronger.

The marble face took life once more,
The stone then fell to sighing,
She drank of my kisses the fire and heat,
With my warm passion vying.

—THE SPHINX

THE MARBLE VENUS

MADAME, if you ask me who is my favorite
Poet, I who can deny you nothing, must
answer truly, he is none of my own race. Rare
are the singers of Erin, Madame, and their
Castalia is a fountain of tears: whoso drinks of
its sweet sorrow shall never be happy again.
Like the fated one who has heard the Banshee's
wail, that soul shall in the midst of joy feel the
near presence of calamity, a boding at the heart
which nothing can silence. This precious blue
flower of sorrow is proper to the poets of my
beloved Erin. It would not flourish under less
tender and humid skies, for it is born of the
rainbow of her smiles and tears.

But, Madame, I have from my youth read a
mort o' poetry, and have even written a little
myself—indifferent bad, I may admit without a
qualm, since the sin was committed long ago, and
you were the dear occasion of it. Alas! perhaps
it had been better for my peace of mind had I
followed the counsel of my old priestly instruc-
tors, "to avoid all occasions of sin".

17

You know, Madame, that the making of poetry
is no longer in fashion, for many reasons, but
chiefly because the present age is too banal to
inspire or receive it. Meantime we have to deal
with prose, or verse that is jejune and vain.
Have we not good reason to love our sainted
Heinrich, whose prose is better than most English poetry? In truth, if we had not a line of his
verse, his prose, brilliant, various, alive with rare
imagery, sparkling with the treasures of the rich-
est fancy ever given to poet, would serve to crown
him with bays unfading. True, as he himself
said of the gentle Antommarchi, it is a stiletto
rather than a style: but what a relief after the
divine heaviness of Goethe! He struck fiercely,
did our Heinrich, though often he wounded his
own breast; and how deep was his gift of tears!
What he said of another* is truer still of himself:
"He was the petted darling of the pale Goddess
of Tragedy. Once in a fit of wild tenderness she
kissed him as though she would draw his whole
heart through his lips with one long, passionate
kiss. The heart began to bleed, and suddenly
understood all the sorrows of this world, and was
filled with infinite sympathy."

* Sterne.

To know our Heine, Madame, is to renew one's faith in the old Greek mythology—a system in which the aristocracy of mind is finely manifest—and to worship Nature as she was worshipped in the antique world. Nay, this modern Heinrich Heine was but an avatar of the old Hermes—you see, Madame, the initial letter is the same, and yet the discovery is original with me! Heine himself took little care to cloak his divine origin. Life and light and love, while they were granted to him, these were the elements of his religion. Early and late he paid his vows to Venus. His voice was a protest harking back to old Olympus against the new Religion of Pain. Much pain he came to suffer himself, perhaps through the malice of the later Dispensation; but he died as he had lived, a son of the gods. Surely the immortal mind was never stronger in him than when from his "mattress-grave," where he lay half blind and paralyzed, his unconquered spirit sent forth this message, matchless in its pathos and irony:

"What avails it me that enthusiastic youths and maidens crown my marble bust with laurel, when the withered hands of an aged nurse are pressing a poultice of Spanish flies behind my ears? What avails it me that all the roses of Shiraz glow and waft incense for me? Alas! Shiraz is two thousand miles from the Rue d'Amsterdam where in the wearisome loneliness of my sick room I get no scent, except it be, perhaps, the perfume of warmed towels. Alas! God's satire weighs heavy on me. The great Author of the Universe, the Aristophanes of Heaven, was bent on demonstrating with crushing force to me the little, earthly, German Aristophanes, how my wittiest sarcasms were only pitiful attempts at jesting in comparison with his, and how miserably I am beneath him in humor, in colossal mockery!"

It is strange, Madame, how godly men pointed the finger of condemnation at the stricken Poet, putting the Christian anathema upon him. Our poor Hermes was having *his* Passion, and the sight of his agonies filled the pietists with rapture. In mediæval times, still regretted in some centres of Christian instruction as the true ages of faith, there was a breed of zealots called flagellants, who used to run madly over Europe, beating themselves—and murdering the Jews. How little essential change has taken place in the religious spirit! Now Heine hated this spirit with a hatred bequeathed to him by generations of his hunted and suffering race, that is to say, like a Jew; and he also hated it like the true Hellene he was: so it took what revenge it could upon him. The petty German princelings who put up conductors on their funny little courts and castles to dodge the lightnings of his wit, also furnished some diversion in kind. For this man had written:

"The people have time enough, they are immortal: Kings only are mortal."

"The human spirit has its rights and will not be rocked to sleep by the lullaby of church bells."

"Men will no longer be put off with promissory notes upon Heaven."

The Tryst

MADAME, when I think of my favorite Poet, whom I so love, though of an alien race, there comes to me a vision which I must put into rude and graceless words—ah, how unworthy of him who has painted it for all time with the iris-hued pencil of fancy! I seem to stand on the banks of the blue Rhine, looking over a fair prospect of vine-covered champaign; quaint villages shining in the cheerful sun, alternating with the umbrage of forest; now and again the river flashing its silver upon the sight;—and still farther beyond, a smiling expanse of flower-decked meadow and plain. But in all that beauteous picture my fancy seeks a little garden, tangled and over-grown with grasses and wild flowers, where the gardener's care has not been felt for many a day. There, in its most neglected and obscure corner, when the moon is risen, I see the cold pure gleam of marble; a broken statue of the antique Venus, fallen from its pedestal and lying half buried under leaves and vines. And see, while I wait, there comes with fearful, faltering step, a boy whose pale young face is fixed with the resolve of a strange passion. Ah me! what ghostly tryst is this? Casting a swift glance around, he flings himself upon his knees beside the fallen Queen of Love and kisses the silent marble lips, murmuring broken words which are not for me to hear. Rising, the solemn stars look upon a face transfigured by destiny and the sacrament of the Ideal.

A nightingale sings . . . .

Now I see a youth leaving the gates of an ancient city. With knapsack on shoulder he trudges away joyously, as one to whom life opens its fairest promise. It is the boy of the deserted garden, but older grown, and with a light in his eyes that owes nothing to the flight of years. Gaily he begins his journey, Nature bidding him on with her eternal smile that only the young understand. Oh, never has she companioned a more memorable pilgrim! But soft! the poet's heart within him speaks: "It is the first of May, and spring is pouring a foam of white blossoms like a sea of life over the earth. Green, the color of hope, is everywhere around me. Everywhere flowers are blooming like beautiful miracles, and my heart will bloom again also. This heart is likewise a flower of strange and wondrous sort.

It is no modest violet, no smiling rose, no pure lily which a maiden may cherish in her white bosom; which withers to-day and blooms again to-morrow. No, this heart rather resembles that strange heavy flower from the woods of Brazil which, according to the legend, blooms but once in a century. . . . No, Agnes, this flower blooms not often, nor without effort, but now it moves, and swells, and bursts in my bosom. . . . My love has burst its bud and shoots upward in eternal dithyrambs of poesy and joy!" . . .

AFTER an interval I see the wayfarer again, pausing at a stately old house in Hamburg, where kind welcome is given him; kindest greeting of all by a fair young girl whose dove-like eyes, mirroring a truthful soul, rest upon him with a certain pity. Ah, how he trembles at her most careless touch, how his glance follows her every motion, and when she is passive, rivets itself upon her like a devotee before a shrine!

They are in a deep garden, these two, where the scent of flowers is heavy on the air. It is a sweet hour, breathing yet the full fragrance of a perfect day. But the moon mounting up sends a long arrow of light across the shimmering foliage, touching the girl's pale cheek with the pure glory of marble. The youth has taken her hands while she turns away her head, as if loath to hear his impassioned speech. These words at length float to me on the garden scents, bringing death in life and an immortal despair to one that hears—"I love, I love thee, Cousin Amalie. And what sayest thou to me?"

"Alas, Cousin, it must not be!" . . .

A nightingale sings.

Adieu!

THE years take wing with the swiftness of a
dream, and now I stand in a great hall filled with
the trophies of art gathered from all ages and
climes to make the priceless spoil of an imperial
city. Everywhere the divinity of marble, pulse-
less and serene, while beyond these sacred walls
the din of vulgar life rises impertinent. And lo!
there in sovereign state, upon a lofty pedestal, I
see the antique Venus of the neglected garden
by the Rhine, where the boy kept his tryst with
the Ideal. The divinities make no sign, but well
I know her for the same that in old time with
many a witching guise succored her mortal son
Æneas.

Quid natum totiens, crudelis tu quoque,
Falsis ludis imaginibus?

Her beauteous arms are gone, that erst en-
circled gods and godlike men, yet as the past was
hers, the future shall be also. Time has wrought
her this maim, jealous of her superior sway, and
she has suffered other wrongs from the barbari-
ans who have sacked Olympus, building upon the

ruins of the old fanes their cross-bearing temples that last but a thousand years: yet is she still divinely content, though her shrines have long been dust and Paphos with all its rosy rites is become a name. For her rule endureth ever in the hearts of men.

And if you ask a proof, see now that haggard, broken man who drags himself wearily to the feet of the immortal Goddess. It is he, the youth of long ago, who kissed her marble lips and gave his soul unto her keeping. Alas! how cruelly have the years dealt with him: yet he looks up to her with a rapture of unchanged worship and love. O miracle of faith, in which the finite rises to the Infinite, the mortal blends with the Immortal!—see how she returns his gaze, with a fulness of divine compassion, as if to say:

"Thou seest I have no arms and may not help thee!"

Then instantly methought the walls and statues vanished, leaving these two alone in the garden where I first saw them . . . .

And a nightingale sang!

PART II

LIFE OF HEINE

WE do not seize an idea, but the idea seizes us and whips us to the arena where we, gladiators perforce, must fight for it!

—HEINE

HEINRICH HEINE

I

CHILDHOOD AND YOUTH

HEINRICH HEINE was born December 12, 1799, in the city of Düsseldorf on the Rhine. For a long time the accepted date of his birth was January 1, 1800, and the poet refused to correct the error, saying he was unquestionably one of the first men of the Nineteenth century. Also let it be set down here, he was born a Jew—a statement which would have sounded worse then than it does now, though in this culminating Christian age there is still room for improvement. But let us give thanks—all of us, Jews and Gentiles: we have come a long way!

Heine imbibed in his cradle and during his early years a full share of the Juden-Schmerz, the great sorrow of Israel. One of his biographers describes him as "in soul an early Hebrew, in spirit an ancient Greek, in mind a republican of the Nineteenth century". There is an apostasy to be charged to him—of which we shall speak later on—and it must be admitted that, Jew himself, he did not spare his own race the scorpion sting of his sarcasm. But a Jew he was in his better moods, in his seasons of calm and power; and a Jew he remained to the last. It is good to recall here his noble confession: "The writer of these lines may be proud that his ancestors came of the noble House of Israel, that he is a descendant of the martyrs who gave a God and a moral code to the world, and who have fought and suffered on every battlefield of thought*."

HEINE'S childish years and boyhood were as happy as those of a poet should be. Of this enchanted period he has left us a characteristic and delightful record. Indeed, Heine has told the story so well that no one may presume to tell it after him without borrowing the poet's own words. For the old German Fatherland, however its political systems might provoke his scathing irony, for his native city of Düsseldorf, he kept during his long exile in after years, the

---

* When one's ancestors in ages beyond recollection killed stags, the descendant still finds pleasure in this legitimate occupation. But my ancestors did not belong to the hunters so much as to the hunted.—THE NORTH SEA.

tenderest affection. His mind was at home on
the Seine; his heart on the Rhine. There, as he
wittily said, were seven towns to dispute the
honor of being his birthplace—Schilda, Krähwinkel, Polkwitz, Bockum, Dülken, Göttingen
and Schoppenstadt. There his poet soul first
awoke to life and love and beauty. There he
lisped that musical German speech which his
genius was to fuse into lyric forms that will keep
his memory alive in German hearts so long as
the Rhine shall run its course toward the sea.

Heine's father, Samson Heine, was an amiable, handsome man, and the poet always pre-
served a loving recollection of him; but, like
most great men, he was his mother's son. What
lover of the poet needs to be told much of the
"old woman who lives by the Dammthor*"; or
of the mutual love extending over so many years,
unchilled, unchanged; or of the tender decep-
tion which the stricken poet practised from his
mattress-grave, keeping her in ignorance of his
awful fate? To me it is the finest chapter in
Heine's life, the one to which we turn for rest
when wearied with his constant feuds, brilliantly
as he fought them.

* One of the gates of Hamburg.

Heine's mother had been a Miss Betty von Geldern. She might have made a better marriage in a worldly way, but it would hardly have resulted in so good a poet. She deserved well of her gifted son and he of her. She brought him into the world; he immortalized her. Mother Heine lived a hundred years before the New Woman, and yet she made few mistakes. One of these was, however, rather serious—that Heinrich could, would or should be anything save a poet. Having been well educated herself—she read Latin, I fear, better than the New Woman —Mother Heine followed with eager interest the growth of her son's mind. "She played the chief part in my development," he tells us; "she made the programme of all my studies, and, even before my birth, began her plans for my education." There were other children to divide her care, but her darling was the eldest born, the glory of whose genius she lived to see, and whom at last she followed to the grave.

Literature, regarded as a profession, was held in small favor by the Heine family, and especially by Uncle Salomon Heine, the great banker of Hamburg, of whom we hear so much in the life-story of the poet. Uncle Salomon, indeed— although he helped Heinrich from time to time and never wholly abandoned him, except in making his will—esteemed the first lyrist of Germany as little better than the fool of the family. There was another uncle on the mother's side, Simon von Geldern, who seems to have had a literary turn, and who gave the young poet much secret encouragement. Having little money to back his opinions, Uncle Simon was distinctly inferior as a moral force to Uncle Salomon; and, therefore, he for the most part, kept his heretical views to himself. But the Muse of Literary History has done tardy justice to the poor relation, and Uncle Simon von Geldern will always have his place in the chronicle.

However, I am inclined to think more kindly of Salomon Heine than are some of the poet's biographers. It is scarcely a just cause of reproach that Uncle Salomon, the Jew prince of Hamburg (as he was called) should have rated commercial values so high and literary values so low. He had known the Ghetto, with its privations, its galling humiliations, its degrading stigma of inferiority. Rising at length by his own exertions to wealth and power, it was hardly to be expected that he should view with tolerance the adoption of so unlucrative a pursuit as poetry by a member of his family. Yet, as I have said, though he looked askance at his scribbling, ne'er-do-well-nephew, he never absolutely gave him the cold shoulder. The provocation was often strong enough, I promise you. Once Heinrich went over to London on a sightseeing tour, Uncle Salomon furnishing the needful. Besides an allowance for travelling expenses, Uncle Salomon entrusted the poet with a draft for £400, which Heinrich was on no account to cash, but merely to preserve and if need were, exhibit, as establishing the credit of the family. Heinrich never could be got to look at money in that way. His rule through life was to spend his money and every other good thing as soon as he came into possession of it—often indeed, by anticipation; so you may be sure it didn't take him long to realize on the valuable bit of paper. Uncle Salomon was furious, and I fancy many a Christian uncle would not have spared his wrath in a like extremity. To his angry and just reproaches the "fool of the family" coolly answered: "My dear uncle, do you really expect to have to pay nothing for the honor of bearing my name?"

II

HISTORY IN ACTION

HEINE very early felt the French influence
which became so controlling an element in
his political philosophy and which gave so decided a bent to his literary genius. History put
on her seven-league boots while little Heinrich
played by the Düssel, or in the green alleys of the
Schlossgarten. Just a month before the poet was
born, in the memorable year 1799, his great hero
Napoleon had achieved his famous *coup d'état*
of the 18th Brumaire. The Revolution knelt
before its master, and then history-making pro-
ceeded in earnest. In 1806—Heinrich is now
seven years old and the First Consul is Emperor
—Duke William took leave of the Duchy of
Berg and the dashing Joachim Murat entered
as Regent. The Rhine Confederation had been
formed and the German States beaten one after
another. Indeed, so many great events were hap-
pening at this time—History paying off her ar-

rears—that a clear head has much ado to follow
them in their right order and relation. Happily
that is not our present business. Amid all this
marching and counter-marching, *allons*-ing and
alliancing, bayoneting and bulleting, partition-
ing and protocolizing, little Heinrich played
with his mates in the quaint streets of Düsseldorf,
or at home tumbled over his toy castles as mer-
rily as the French armies busy at the same work
in kind.

But one never-to-be-forgotten day the statue
of the Elector Jan Wilhelm was missed from the
town square, and the French troops marched in,
the "drum-major throwing his gold-knobbed
baton as high as the first story", while the
drunken cripple Gumpertz rolled in the gutter,
singing:

Ça ira! Ça ira!

A wonderful day that was to the little boy, his
eager heart aflame with the new marvel of all
this fanfare and soldiering. And wonderful days
were to come, listening to Monsieur LeGrand,
the French tambour—"so long billeted upon us,
who looked like a very devil and yet was such
an angelic character and such an incomparable
drummer!" We all know how he taught the
young Heinrich with his rat-a-tat-tat some les-

sons of modern history in which he, the brave
LeGrand, had borne a part; and we have been
glad to learn in our turn. Nay, we may yet
hearken with pleasure to the recitals of Monsieur
LeGrand.

"I saw the march across the Simplon, the Emperor in front, with the brave Grenadiers climb-
ing up behind, while the startled eagles screamed
and the glaciers thundered in the distance; I saw
the Emperor clasping the standard on the bridge
of Lodi; I saw the Emperor in his gray cloak at
Marengo; I saw the Emperor on horseback at
the battle of the Pyramids—nothing but smoke
and Mamelukes; I saw the Emperor at Auster-
litz—twing! how the bullets whizzed over the
smooth ice! I saw, I heard the battle of Jena—
dum, dum, dum—I saw, I heard the battles of
Eylau, Wagram—no, I could hardly stand it.
Monsieur LeGrand drummed till my own ear-
drum was nearly cracked."

But a more wonderful day was yet to come, for
History was all the time getting on in her seven-
league boots. Every day, nay, every hour, the
French were upsetting boundaries and generally
making havoc with the established order. As in
the fairy tale, the Giant—that is, the people,—
had awakened from his enchanted sleep, and the

whole world was magically in motion. Murat, the bold Joachim, exchanged his spurs for the crown of Naples. This was in 1808. King Joachim thereupon ceded the Duchy of Berg to his lord and master, Napoleon, who transferred it to his brother, Louis, King of Holland. The pendulum was swinging back and the reign of liberty and equality was producing royalties with a vengeance. But some good came out of all this, and especially to the long persecuted Jews. (We are not to forget that Heine was himself a Jew.) In 1812 the Code Napoleon was extended to the German provinces under the French influence. The mists of the Middle Ages took flight. The Ghettos gave up their ghost.

drunken Gumpertz bellowed, and the people shouted with a thousand voices, 'Long live the Emperor!'"

NAPOLEON'S wonderful career inspired the greatest writers of his era, and in truth his influence was not exhausted up to the middle of the last century; it was as provocative to Heine, who called himself a son of the Revolution, as to his friend and contemporary Balzac, who seems unable to keep the Corsican out of his pages. A little before it had challenged the genius of Byron to some of his boldest and happiest efforts, the great English poet making no secret of his Napoleon-idolatry. Byron indeed lampooned Wellington quite as savagely as did Heine, and he was wont to boast that Bonaparte and himself were the only two public characters in Europe who possessed the same initials: N. B.— (Noel Byron.) All of which aroused English prejudice against Byron, and he is not forgiven unto this day.

As we have seen, Heine found a constantly fruitful source of inspiration in the Napoleonic theme, the passion seizing him in early youth and lasting well into middle age. But none of his writings on the Napoleon epos has more

pleasingly identified him with the popular
legend of the Man of Destiny than his ballad of
"The Two Grenadiers". Indeed, there are few
things more famous in the entire cycle of Napoleonic literature. The following version exhibits
at least the vigor and contagious sentiment of
the original, written, be it noted, in Heine's
fifteenth year.

To France were travelling two grenadiers,
From prison in Russia returning,
And when they came to the German frontiers,
They hung down their heads in mourning.

There came the heart-breaking news to their
    ears
That France was by fortune forsaken;
Scattered and slain were her brave grenadiers,
And Napoleon, Napoleon was taken!

Then wept together those two grenadiers
O'er their country's departed glory;
"Woe's me," cried one, in the midst of his tears,
"My old wound,—how it burns at the story!"

Said the other, "Alas, the end is come,
What avails any longer living?

Yet have I a wife and child at home,
For an absent father grieving."

"Who cares for wife?   Who cares for child?
Dearer thoughts in my bosom awaken;
Go beg, wife and child, when with hunger wild,
For Napoleon, Napoleon is taken!

"Oh, grant me, brother, my only prayer,
When in death my eyes are closing:
Take me to France, and bury me there;
In France be my ashes reposing.

"This cross of the Legion of Honor bright,
Let it lie, near my heart, upon me;
Give me my musket in my hand,
And gird my sabre on me.

"So will I lie, and arise no more,
My watch like a sentinel keeping,
Till I hear the cannon's thundering roar,
And the squadrons above me sweeping.

"Then the Emperor comes! and his banners
    wave,
With their eagles o'er him bending;
And I will come forth, all in arms, from my
    grave,
Napoleon, Napoleon attending!"

IV

RED SEFCHEN

LOVE awakens the poet—and Heine was to be lover and poet all his days.

He was in his sixteenth year when he had his first taste of the Eden-apple of passion; and about the same time he fell ill of his first poems. Something like this has happened to many a man, and the story were trite and scarce worth the hearing had we not to deal with a poet of Heine's magnitude.

Heine's experiences, as he relates them, seem like fortunate inventions; we are bound to envy them, even though we keep telling ourselves that the charm is all in the art of the narrator.

Thus it is with the story of his first love Josepha ("red Sefchen") who laid her hand upon the poet in his breast and roused him to his first consciousness of the two great passions of his life—Love and Poetry. This tale he told many, many years afterward when he lay nailed

46

to his mattress-grave in Paris, and if you will read it in the poet's own words you will believe with me that it is of the very essence of his power and genius.

I must tell it very briefly and in my own graceless words, though the biographers of Heine as a rule do not scruple to borrow from him; competition being out of the question.

Josepha, barely sixteen but slender and tall for her years, was the red-haired niece of the Woman of Goch, a reputed witch and dabbler in the occult, who had come to live at Düsseldorf in Heine's boyhood. They were Jews and of an infamously low grade, the men of the family having filled for several generations the ab-horred office of public executioner. Thus the women were sufficiently branded and stigma-tized in public regard even without the vulgar cantrips of *die Göchin*. It seems the execu-tioners were all dead now by warrant of time, and the women kept a great sword which had long served officially in the family line of busi-ness, and which was said to have taken the lives of one hundred criminals. Not very proper persons for Master Heine to know, nor was the house of the Woman of Goch, bedlamite and witch, a desirable school of morals and good breeding.

But Josepha was of a singular beauty, with her marble face, red curved lips, rather long white teeth, great dark eyes, and slim shapely figure, "like a statue in a wet garment". And above all she had red hair that she drew in thick braids about her neck, so that it sometimes seemed as if the life blood were welling from her throat. When the devil wishes to make a woman seductive beyond the ordinary, he adds red hair as his culminating effect. Needless to stop here and recall the ravages it has wrought all down the cycles of time. But the reader will bethink himself that red-haired Jewish women are very scarce—even the Shulamite, beloved of Solomon, lacked this sovereign appanage of beauty. And as there is red hair and hair that is red, it is needful to mention that Josepha's was of that particular hue and shade which men have gone mad about since they first began to pay any attention to women. Parenthetically I may add that the most successful heroines in fiction are those described as having warm-colored tresses.

Josepha had this wonderful red hair tied about her white throat one day when young

Heine called and the Woman of Goch happened luckily to be from home. They played amorously yet fearfully with their love, as is the way of the young, unskilled in these early pitfalls of passion. Heine remarks that her voice—husky and sweet at the same time—was like his in tone, and often startled him with the resemblance. But what lover has not made the same observation? This naïveté of Heine is one of the most artless yet profoundly artful things in his repertory. Here it gives just the touch which convinces us of this wild young passion. The lovers joked and smiled, sighed and dallied, and then the boy poet dared Sefchen to bring forth the sword of the hundred dead. And here I must positively yield the cue—there are no words but his in which to narrate the sequel:

"I had not long to ask, and she went to the room (where it was kept) and came back with a monstrous sword which she swung mightily, in spite of the weakness of her arms, whilst she sang, half in menace and half in roguery:

'Wilt thou kiss the naked sword
That is given by the Lord?'

"And in the same tone of voice I replied: 'I

will not kiss the bright, bright sword—I will kiss red Sefchen!' and as she could not withstand me from fear of hurting me with the fatal steel, she had to let me kiss her; and very warmly I laid hands on her slender hips and kissed her scornful mouth. Yes, in spite of the executioner's sword with which a hundred poor rascals had been beheaded, and in spite of the infamy incurred by those who came in contact with any of the despised race, I kissed the lovely daughter of the executioner."

Heine tells us nothing more about his love for red Sefchen, and we are piqued to know her subsequent fate and future—with that wonder· ful red hair! Perhaps she had abundantly fulfilled her destiny in awakening the greatest of modern lyrists. Yet as the shadows close about her fantastic lovely figure, so soon withdrawn from the poet's life, we think of her with a certain tenderness and regret.

Even so, Josepha remains: her influence is plain to be seen and felt in Heine's first poems, the "Dream Pictures"—surely the most wonderful first book of so young a poet in the annals of literature. She used to sing weird folk-songs to him that roused his nascent fancy and imagination. Once she wrote down for him, in her blood, a verse about the wicked old sword (a true niece of the Woman of Goch, you perceive!) He lost it, he tells us, but perhaps Sefchen knew better:—it is written forever in the first poems of Heinrich Heine.

V

AMALIE

NOT long after the Josepha episode, Heine's family thought to decide his vocation for him, and so he was sent to Frankfort-on-Main, where there was a ghetto, the sweet relish of which the poet never forgot.

He stayed there only a few weeks, and then Uncle Salomon, at Hamburg, tried his hand at making something other than a poet out of his nephew. Had Uncle Salomon possessed a little more imagination, he might have spared himself a humiliating failure. It was impossible to drum the commercial ABC into Heinrich's wayward head. Even his watch, as he tells us, had a habit of going wrong and getting into the hands of the Jews. To make matters worse, the graceless youth, for whose future Uncle Salomon would not have given a sixpence, committed the folly of falling in love with Uncle Salomon's beautiful daughter, Amalie. If

Heine's cousin had been a less prudent and sensible girl, we should probably have lost a deal of fine poetry, for, of course they would have got married somehow, and Uncle Salomon would have paid the bills until the end of the chapter. But Amalie was much of her father's mind. She gave her cousin small encouragement, and—a more cruel thing—even told him she did not like his poetry. In the end, and that was very soon, she married a young man of approved Hebrew descent and strictly commercial aspirations, whose name I haven't taken the trouble to remember.

The critics and biographers have generally deduced from this little passage in Heine's life that he carried through all the after years an incurable wound of the heart. It is vastly unpopular to doubt this, and ungallant in the bargain; but, though Heine suffered acutely from the disappointment of his first pure love, and though it yielded him many a lyric of exquisite pain, I am afraid it argues a misreading of the facts to impute to him a lifelong Wertherian anguish.

Surely the literature of crossed love does not yield a stranger page than the following verses, which were written a year or two after Heine's disappointment. I quote them as an amazing instance of his power to score a poetical effect where only the grotesque seemed possible. In this respect the little poem is quite unique among *vers de société*.

WHEN I met one day on a journey
　My sweetheart's relations by chance,
Small sister and father and mother,
　They recognized me at a glance.

They asked if my health was better,
　And at once began to exclaim
That, except for being paler,
　I looked exactly the same.

I asked after aunts and cousins,
　And many a family bore;
And after the little puppy
　Whose bark was so gentle of yore.

I offered congratulations,
　Lisping stock phrases inane;
I desired my kindest remembrance
　To *her,* again and again.

Small sister meanwhile was shrilling:
　"The puppy so gentle and small
Grew big and awfully savage,
　And was drowned in the Rhine, after all."

The little one's like my darling:
   And when she laughs I see
The self-same eyes whose sweetness
   Has brought such woe to me!

That it was a genuine feeling, however, cannot be doubted, in spite of the "compensations" which Heine subsequently allowed himself; in spite also of that ancient difficulty, the confounding of emotion with the literary impulse. Heine needed to sing quite as much as he needed to love, and from his first heart-grief he drew his most poignant inspiration, that which of all his work the world still seeks with unabated eagerness. But the Amalie-sorrow never quite died out of Heine's heart, and I think he never came to laugh at it. When the wound was fresh and green he wrote:

ALL of my days are poisoned—
How could it otherwise be?
The bloom of my very existence
Hast thou e'en poisoned for me.

All of my days are poisoned—
How could it otherwise be?
In my bosom I've many a serpent;
There too, my love, I have thee!

And when it was healed over by the long lapse
of years, with the pain of it forgotten under other
losses and sorrows, he could write in one of the
last of his poems:

THOU wert a blonde-haired maid without a stain,
So neat, so prim, so cool!   I stayed in vain
To see thy bosom's guarded gates unroll,
And Inspiration breathe upon thy soul.

On hills with vineyards' clambering leafage gay,
Glassed in the Rhine, we roamed one summer
    day;
Bright was the sun, and from the shining cup
Of every flower a giddy scent flew up.

A kiss of fire, a deep voluptuous blush,
Burned on each pink and every rosy bush,
Ideal flames in dandelions glowed,
And lit each sorriest weed that edged our road.

But thou went'st on with even-stepping feet,
Clad in white satin, elegant and neat;
No child of Netcher's brush more trim and nice,
And in thy stays a little heart of ice.

VI

THE APOSTASY

LEAVING Hamburg, with this bitter-sweet memory and finding in his sense of grief and loss, food for the lyrical impulse now maturing with his powers, Heine returned home to prepare himself for a profession. He entered the University of Bonn in 1819.

Napoleon being now at St. Helena, the hand was set back on the clock. So far as lay in its power, the Holy Alliance had undone the work of the Revolution. A Jew might not practise the profession of law—no profession, indeed, save medicine—in the Kingdom of Prussia; so nothing was left for Heine but to apostatize or lay aside his ambition—which indeed was rather that of his family—to become *doctor juris*. Urged by his relatives and friends (who saw no harm in thus evading a barbarous proscription) he chose the former alternative. For this he has been unsparingly, though it seems to me unjustly, condemned

by the rigorists of his own race. Heine himself
affected to regard lightly the circumstance of his
quasi-conversion to Lutheranism.* With incomparable irony he tells us: "That I became a
Christian is the fault of those Saxons who
changed sides so suddenly at Leipzig; or else of
Napoleon who need never have gone to Russia;
or of the schoolmaster who taught him geog-
raphy at Brienne and neglected to tell him that
it was cold in Moscow in winter; if Montalem-
bert became minister and could drive me away
from Paris, I would turn Catholic. *Paris vaut
bien une messe!†*"

Within a very few years the enlightened government of Prussia paid this notable convert to
the state religion the handsome compliment of
interdicting his books. It is certain that Heine
always bitterly regretted the concession he had
made to a mediæval prejudice. However lightly
one may hold a traditional faith, one may choose
an easier method of parting with it than by an
act of formal and public apostasy. No man
cared less than Heine for the anathemas of other
men, yet he remained keenly sensitive to reproaches on this score. The degree of *doctor*

* See Heine on Religion—Part III.
† "Paris is well worth one Mass."

juris which cost him so dear brought him nothing. It was from Göttingen, by the way, he received this learned distinction—Göttingen which he has visited with some of the happiest strokes of his satirical genius.

Heine was a brilliant but irregular student. He was reading and rhyming poetry when he ought to have been busy with the Pandects.

So acute and native is the quality of his wit that the chronicle of his student days may be read to-day with interest as fresh as when it was first given to the world. Horace's *qualis ab incepto* is eminently true of Heine—he seems to have begun at once with an assured and individual style.

Prosing with professors over the Justinian Code came to an end at last. In his doctoral thesis Heine made a slip on the noun *caput*—the thesis was, of course, in Latin—and always remembered it with a twinge—which shows he was not entirely devoid of the pedantry of the place that he has so amusingly satirized. He had previously been rusticated from the University on account of a duel—his personal courage was then and ever after undoubted—and the pundits of the institution looked with small favor on the poetizing young Jew. Yet in the realm of let-

ters, Göttingen is, and ever will be, better known
from the residence of Heine than from any other
circumstance in its venerable history. Hegel, by
the way, owes to Heine the sole humorous association with his name.* To the readers of the
Harzreise I need not recall the famous description of the town of Göttingen, "celebrated for its
sausages and University"; or the happy application of the term Philistine, which has passed into
universal currency.

It was in 1824 that Heine shook the dust of
Göttingen from his feet and carried away much
of its learned dust in his brain. Three years
earlier his great idol Napoleon had died at St.
Helena—"the saviour of the world" (was
Heine's characteristic comment) "who suffered
under Hudson Lowe, as it is written in the gos-
pels of Las Casas, of O'Meara and of Antom-
marchi†." And with what is perhaps the bit-
terest stroke of his unequalled irony, he added:
"Strange, the greatest adversaries of the Emperor have already found an awful fate. Lon-

* *Vide* German Philosophers—Part III.

† He censured Sir Walter Scott's dull and belittling
history of Napoleon as "a blasphemy in twelve volumes",
and declared that the great romancer's fame was buried
with it.

donderry* cut his throat; Louis the 18th rotted on his throne, and Professor Saalfeld is still professor at Göttingen!"

* Better known to English readers as Viscount Castle-reagh, the chief agent of Pitt in effecting the Union of Great Britain and Ireland.

VII

JUDEN-SCHMERZ

SEVEN years, rich with the outpouring of his genius, followed from the day Heine left the classic precincts of Göttingen until he turned his face toward France and Paris. In the interval he had, in spite of the reigning sovereignty of the great Goethe, established his title as the first lyric poet of Germany.

Heine was proud to call himself a son of the Revolution, and such he was, in poetic as well as political impulse. But he was also a son of the free Rhine and would make good his claim to the title. No man more fully appreciated the sacrifices made by the French people in the cause of human liberty. As a Jew, the descendant of a hated and persecuted race, he felt a special obligation of gratitude.

Criticism can take no account of the blemishes in Heine's character as a German or as a Jew. The measure of his literary accomplishment raises him above these things. This is the more just since Heine as a poet is eminently cosmopolitan. The note of provinciality is not in him. And this distinction belongs only to poets of the first class.

Notwithstanding, it is of great interest to study Heine in his relations of sympathy, his spiritual or racial touch with his own people. I have said that he shared deeply in the Juden-Schmerz, the great sorrow of Israel. "The history of the Jews," he tells us, "is tragical, and yet if one were to write about this tragedy, he would be laughed at. This is the most tragic of all!"

Heine wrote much and variously on this subject, constantly recurring to it, now with the broadest comic humor, now with awful pathos, and again dissembling his own pain with bitter irony, as in his note on Shakespeare's Shylock:

"I, at least a wandering dreamer of dreams, looked round me on the Rialto to see if I could find Shylock. I had something to tell him that would have pleased him—which was that his cousin Monsieur de Shylock in Paris, had become the proudest baron in all Christendom * and had received from their Catholic Majesties the Order of Isabella, which was originally estab-

* *Vide* Note C—Part III.

lished to celebrate the expulsion of the Jews and Moors from Spain. But I found him not on the Rialto, so I determined to look for my old acquaintance in the synagogue.

"Though I looked all round in the synagogue of Venice, I could nowhere see his face. And yet it seemed to me he must be there, praying more fervently than any of his fellow-believers with stormy, wild passion—yea, with madness!— to the throne of Jehovah, the severe, divine Monarch. I saw him not. But toward evening, when according to the belief of the Jews, the gates of Heaven are closed and no further prayer can enter, I heard a voice in which tears flowed as they were never wept from human eyes. There was a sobbing which might have moved a stone to pity—there were utterances of agony such as could only come from a heart which held within itself all the martyrdom that an utterly tormented race had endured for eighteen centuries. It was the death-rattle of a soul which nearing its death, sinks to the ground before the gates of Heaven. And this voice seemed to be well known to me— as if I had heard it long, long ago, when it wailed just as despairingly, 'Jessica, my child!' "

Now for the other mood, and let us not forget that with Heine the mood of the moment is supreme. We have but to take what the gods give us and be thankful. Also the strange mingling of irony, truth, humor and pathos is the chief mark of our poet's genius—the one thing in which he is least imitable.

"There lives at Hamburg, in a one-roomed lodging in the Baker's Broad Walk, a man whose name is Moses Lump. All the week he goes about in the rain and wind, with his pack on his back, to earn his few shillings. But when on Friday night he comes home, he finds the candle-stick with seven candles lighted, and the table covered with a fine, white cloth. And he puts away from him his pack and his cares, and he sits down to table with his squinting wife, and yet more squinting daughter, and eats fish with them—fish that has been dressed in beautiful white garlic sauce; says therewith the grandest psalms of King David; rejoices with his whole heart over the deliverance of the Children of Israel out of Egypt; rejoices, too, that all the wicked ones who have done hurt to the Children of Israel have ended by taking themselves off; that King Pharaoh, Nebuchadnezzar, Haman, Antiochus, Titus, and all such villains are dead, while he, Moses Lump, is yet alive and eating fish with his wife and daughter! He contemplates his candles with satisfaction, but on no account will he snuff them for himself. And I can tell you, if the candles burn a little dim, and the snuffers-woman, whose business it is to snuff them, is not at hand, and if Rothschild the Great were at that moment to come in—with his brokers, bill-discounters, agents, and chief clerks with whom he conquers the world—and were to say, 'Moses Lump, ask me what favor you will and it shall be granted,'—I am convinced Moses Lump would quietly answer, 'Rothschild, snuff me those candles!' And Rothschild the Great would exclaim, 'If I were not Rothschild, I would be Moses Lump!'"

VIII

THE POET-LIBERATOR

HEINE'S political sense was as sane and shrewd as his wit was keen. He has given us no better example of it than the following:

"An Englishman loves Freedom as he loves his lawfully wedded wife. He regards her as a possession, and if he does not treat her with special tenderness, yet, if need be, he knows how to defend her. A Frenchman loves Freedom as he does his chosen bride; he will commit a thousand follies for her sake. A German loves Freedom as he does his old grandmother. And yet, after all, no one can tell how things may turn out. The grumpy Englishman, in an ill temper with his wife, is capable some day of putting a rope around her neck. The inconstant Frenchman may become unfaithful to his adored mistress and be seen fluttering about the Palais Royal after another. But the German will never quite abandon his old grandmother. He will always keep for her a nook by the chimney corner where she may tell her fairy tales to the listening children."

Save the Chinese, no people have excelled the Germans in attachment to the idea of kingship by divine right, with its related blessing of a hereditary aristocracy. It is still believed that such is the form of government most acceptable in the sight of Heaven, where once the socialists and republicans under Lucifer caused a serious insurrection, which was put down only after the greatest trouble by Michael, first of all legitimists. Hence the peculiar favor with which the good Lord is supposed to regard those earthly governments patterned upon the model established by Himself.

This was a favorite theme with our poet, who hated dulness and pretence, stupidity and intolerance wherever he found them, but most bitterly of all in the trappings of prescriptive authority. No stronger proof of German passivity could be adduced than that it seems to have withstood even the poisoned shafts of Heine's satire and ridicule.

It is, however, not unusual to find the spirit of revolt most keenly alive under a general appearance of submission and compliance; so we need not doubt that there were hearts in Germany which eagerly treasured up Heine's burning words against the mediæval body-of-death under which the nation lay—alas! for the greater part, still lies.*

Never did our poet preach the new gospel of democracy with keener effect than in the following story taken, as he says, out of the life of Charles V.†

"The poor Emperor was taken prisoner by his enemies and thrown into a wretched prison. I think it was in the Tyrol. He sat alone there in all his wretchedness, forsaken by all his knights and his courtiers, and no one came to help him. I do not know if in those days he had the curd-white face with which Holbein represents him in his pictures. But that prominent under-lip, the sign of a disdain for mankind, was then, undoubtedly, more protruding than in his pictures. He had good cause to despise the people who had fluttered so devotedly around him in the sunshine of his good fortune, and who left him solitary in his obscurity and distress. Suddenly the

* As written in 1911. Whatever the costs and misfortunes of the Great War, 1914-1918, it is impossible that Germany should ever revert to former conditions.

† Or, as the French version more correctly has it, "from the life of the Emperor Maximilian."

prison door opened, and a cloaked man entered, and when the cloak was thrown aside the King recognized his faithful Kunz von der Rosen, the court fool. This man brought him consolation and advice, and he was the court fool. . . .

" 'Oh, German Fatherland! Oh, dear German people! I am thy Kunz von der Rosen. The man whose peculiar office was to make the time pass for thee, and who only amused thee in thy good days, presses into thy prison in the time of thy misfortune. Here under my cloak, I bring thee thy strongest sceptre, thy beautiful crown. Do you not recognize me, my Emperor? If I cannot free thee, at least will I comfort thee, and thou shalt have some one near thee with whom thou canst speak of thy direful sorrows, one who loves thee and whose best jokes and best blood are at thy service. For thou, my people, art the true Emperor, the rightful lord of thy land. Thy will is sovereign, and far more legitimate than that purple vested *tel est notre plaisir,* which invokes a divine right without any other warrant than the foolish prating of tonsured jugglers. Thy will, my people, is the only rightful source of power. Though thou liest yet in chains, thy right will assert itself at length; the day of thy deliverance approaches, a new era begins. My

Emperor, the night is ended, and out there beyond the rosy glow of morning dawns!'

" 'Kunz von der Rosen, my fool, you deceive yourself. You perchance mistake a glittering axe for the sun, and the morning glow is naught but blood.'

" 'No, my Emperor, it is the sun, though it rises in the west. For six thousand years, it has always risen in the east; it is now full time it should change its course.'

" 'Kunz von der Rosen, my fool, thou hast lost the bells from off thy red cap, and it has now so strange an appearance, that red cap.'

" 'Alas, my Emperor, at the thought of thy misfortunes I shook my head so furiously, that the fool's bells have fallen from my cap; but it is none the worse therefor.'

" 'Kunz von der Rosen, my fool, what breaks and cracks out there?'

" 'Be still! It is the carpenter's saw and axe, and the doors of your prison will soon be open, and you will be free, my Emperor.'

" 'Am I really Emperor? Alas, it is the fool who tells me so!'

" 'Oh, do not sigh, my dear master. The air of the prison renders you fearful; when you are reinstated in your power you will again feel the hardy Emperor-blood coursing through your veins; you will be proud as an emperor, and arrogant, and gracious, and smiling, and ungrateful as princes are.'

" 'Kunz von der Rosen, my fool, when I am once more free, what wilt thou do?'

" 'I will then sew new bells on my cap.'

" 'And how shall I recompense thy fidelity?'

" 'Ah! dear master, do not order me to be killed!' "

IX

PARIS

IN 1831 Heine took a long-meditated step and
crossed the Rhine—the Jordan which, he said,
separates the sacred Land of Freedom (France)
from the Land of the Philistines (Germany).
Beyond the attraction which Paris offered as the
centre of art and taste, the poet was actuated by
other reasons, sufficiently cogent, in leaving the
Fatherland. I have noted how his prose writings had brought him under official censure. It
was not at all unlikely that severer measures
might be preparing for him. He had received a
hint, he tells us, that there were irons in the for-
tress of Spandau which would be uncomfortable
wearing in the winter. No oysters, of which he
was fond, were obtainable there, and there were
no fowl, except flies, which had a habit of falling
into the soup and thus making it more substan-
tial. Moreover, the poet was strongly moved by
the July revolution, in which Louis Philippe, the

Citizen King, succeeded to the Bourbon, Charles the Tenth. The sun in Germany began to look to him like a Prussian cockade. "Oh, the grand week in Paris!" he exclaims. "The spirit of liberty which spread over Germany did, to be sure, sometimes overturn the night-lamps, so that the red hangings of some thrones were singed and the gold crowns grew hot under burning nightcaps. But the old catchpolls in the pay of the police soon brought out their fire-buckets, and they snuff about more watchfully than ever and forge stronger chains. And I notice that invisible walls, thicker than ever, are rising round the German people."

On the second day of May, 1831, he arrived in Paris. His reputation had preceded him, and gained for him the entrée to the first literary circles. Heine was then in his thirty-second year, in the full vigor of health, and so handsome as to win from Théophile Gautier the title of the German Apollo. Among the notables who welcomed the poet to Paris were Meyerbeer, George Sand, Gautier, Michelet, Dumas, Sainte-Beuve, Quinet, Gérard de Nerval, Ludwig Boerne, Schlegel, and Humboldt. Heine's contentment in his new sphere, in the Capital of Intellect far removed from the petty German censors, is best described by his own famous phrase to Ferdinand Hiller, the composer, returning to Germany. "If any of my friends ask about me," he said, "say I feel like a fish in water; or rather, when one fish in the ocean asks another how he is feeling, he gets the answer, 'I feel like Heine in Paris.'"

Heine, a born man of letters, as Matthew Arnold calls him, at once entered upon the second and more important period of his literary career. His letters to German newspapers, his reviews and other prose writings, put him in possession of an assured, if modest, income. There was, besides, an allowance from Uncle Salomon—not a munificent one, indeed, but still useful and acceptable. It is said the poet was also, for a considerable time, in receipt of a pension from the French Government, and the story lent color to some unworthy aspersions cast upon him by his own countrymen. The fact seems to have been that Heine was for a time carried on the list of foreign refugees whom the French Government assisted, through motives of policy.* That the poet never performed a sinister service nor one in any way impeaching his integrity as

* *Vide* Note A—Part III.

a man and a patriot, was long ago made clear to his most invidious critics.

In the account which he drew up concerning his estrangement from Ludwig Börne—his fellow-countryman, and a zealous, if intemperate, patriot—Heine repudiated the charges above noted. "Do you hold out from the grave an imploring hand?" he cries. "I give you mine without malice. See how white and clean it is! It has never been soiled by the clasp of the mob or the gold of the people's enemies."

True, as it is, that Heine seemed to lack stableness of purpose, he at least never abjured his liberal creed. Belonging to the aristocracy of mind, he was yet a leader and a prophet in the great democratic movement. With all his admiration for Napoleon, he was wont to say that he followed him absolutely only up to the 18th Brumaire.* Heine's political vision was marvellously keen and his deductions original and just. Scarcely any portion of his work is more interesting than the political reflections and observations injected into his "History of the Romantic School", his "Religion and Philosophy in Ger-

* Otherwise November 9, 1799 when Bonaparte, on his return from Egypt, made his *coup d'état* and seized upon the sovereign power as First Consul.

many" and sprinkled over his miscellaneous writings.

With his protean humor and fatal facility of satire, it was only to be expected that sooner or later, Heine would give mortal offence to most of his liberal friends, as well as many of his compatriots. The affair with Ludwig Börne, which, after the apostasy, I would rather wipe out than any other passage in Heine's life—drew him into a duel. There were other quarrels, hideously vulgar, and ah, how unworthy of the high-strung, sensitive poet! These are, however, only the shadows in the picture. A curious student may now, perhaps, by an effort recall the names of the men who quarrelled with Heine on the score of backsliding in his political or religious faith. No one can estimate the immense influence which his writings have had in favor of liberal ideas in Germany and throughout the world. Not vainly nor with undue emphasis did he picture his life-long battle with the foes of liberty in his famous poem "Enfant Perdu":

In Freedom's War, of "Thirty Years" and more,
    A lonely outpost have I held—in vain!
With no triumphant hope or prize in store,
    Without a thought to see my home again.

I watched both day and night: I could not sleep
  Like my well-tented comrades far behind,
Though near enough to let their snoring keep
  A friend awake, if e'er to doze inclined.

And thus, when solitude my spirits shook,
  Or fear—for all but fools know fear some-
    times,—
To rouse myself and them, I piped and took
  A gay revenge in all my wanton rhymes.

Yes! there I stood, my musket always ready,
  And when some sneaking rascal showed his
    head,
My eye was vigilant, my aim was steady,
  And gave his brains an extra dose of lead.

But war and justice have far different laws,
  And worthless acts are often done right well;
The rascals' shots were better than their cause,
  And I was hit—and hit again, and fell!

That outpost is abandoned: while the one
  Lies in the dust, the rest in troops depart;
Unconquered—I have done what could be done,
  With sword unbroken, and with broken heart.

X

THE MATTRESS-GRAVE

IN the year 1841 Heine wrote to his sister:
"On the 31st of August I was married to
Mathilde Creszentia Mirat, with whom I have
quarrelled every day these six years." The poet's
union with the amiable Frenchwoman contrib-
uted to the small sum of happiness reserved for
his last years. A terrible and insidious disease,
consumption of the spinal marrow, showed itself
as early as 1845, in a partial paralysis, which
gradually extended over the whole system. Then
in 1848 began for the stricken poet the tragedy of
the mattress-grave, and the crown of an unexampled agony was added to the supreme laurel of
poesy. Even as early as 1846 Heine wrote to his
friend, Heinrich Laube: "If you do not find me
here—faubourg Poissonière No. 41—please look
for me in the cemetery of Montmartre—not in
Père Lachaise, which is too noisy for me."

Our Heinrich was surely no saint, yet his

awful sufferings brought to light in his character unsuspected resources of firmness, sweetness and resignation. His chief anxieties were,
first for his wife, that she should not be left by
his death without a provision; and then, for his
old mother in Germany, the "old woman by the
Dammthor", that she should not learn of his terrible misfortune. His woeful state was for some
time needlessly embittered by the heartless con-
duct of his cousin Carl, who refused to pay an
allowance promised by Uncle Salomon, now
dead, but which the latter had omitted to provide
in his will. Finally Carl yielded the point, but
he first made terms with the poet relative to the
latter's treatment of the Heine family in his
memoirs; and it was further agreed that one-
half of the allowance should be continued to the
poet's widow.*

Dark as was Heine's lot, in those terrible last
years, the solace of his genius remained to him.
With death at his pillow and the sentient world
of light and life and joy shut out from him, his
genius unconquered yet rose to new heights—as
if he would gather fresh laurels to be laid on his
bier. "Like a dead man, the living poet was
nailed in his coffin," writes Théophile Gautier,

* *Vide* "Mathilde" and "Mother Heine"—Part III.

"but when we bent listening over him, we heard poetry ringing from under the pall."

But the poet himself is the best witness of his own agony. Listen:

"My body is so shrunken away that hardly anything but my voice is left, and my bed reminds me of the sounding grave of the enchanter Merlin in the Broceliande forest in Brittany, under the tall oaks whose tops rise like green flames into heaven. Ah, friend Merlin, I envy you those trees, with their cool breezes, for no green leaf flutters over my mattress-grave in Paris."

Again: "I am no more a Hellene of jovial life and portly person, laughing cheerfully down on dismal Nazarenes—only a poor death-sick Jew!"

But not dead yet, no, not dead! For he cries out with the courage of immortal mind—"Though I am sick unto death, my soul has not suffered mortal hurt. It is a drooping and athirst, but not yet withered flower, which still has its roots firmly planted in the ground of truth and love."

And the terrible likeness he found for his affliction in the leper of the "Limburg Chronicle". Hear again: "In 1480, throughout all Germany, songs were sung and whistled that were sweeter and lovelier than any that were ever heard before in the German land. But, says the chronicle, a young priest affected with the leprosy had written these songs, and had withdrawn himself from all the world into a desert. These lepers of the Middle Ages, thrust out from all human intercourse, wandered about, wrapped from head to foot, a hood over their faces, carrying a rattle called a Lazarus bell, with which they gave warning of their approach, so that all might draw aside from the way. Often in my sad visions of the night, I think I see before me the poor priest of the 'Limburg Chronicle', my brother in Apollo, and his suffering eyes gleam strangely from beneath his hood; but in a moment he glides away, and, like the echo of a dream, I hear the sharp tones of the Lazarus bell."

It is a strange picture called up by the sufferings of the poet—his mind triumphing over the decay of his body—his genius marking new achievements—his mordant wit and terrible irony active to the last. The ruling passion, strong even in death, was never more signally illustrated. His last word is a jest: "God will pardon me; *it is his trade!*"

But there is a relief to the tragedy of the mattress-grave, which were else too painful to contemplate.* The cheerfulness of the dying man, the amazing vigor of his mind, the undaunted bravery of his spirit—these may well detain us for a brief space before we turn away from that solemn scene.

To the doctor who asked him if he could whistle, using the French word which means also to hiss (*siffler*), the poet gasped, "Alas, no! not even a comedy of M. Scribe's". When Berlioz, the composer, came to see him, shortly before the end, the poet exclaimed, "What! a visitor! Berlioz was always original!" And the good-natured Mathilde, often made the sport of his playful humor, contented herself with saying, placidly: "Very well, my dear, have your joke, but you know you can not do without me."

Once his Nonotte, as he called her, went out for a drive, and was gone so long that the poet pretended his first thought was that she had eloped from her sick husband with some cunning Lothario. Then he sent the nurse to her room to see if Cocotte, her pet parrot, was there. Yes, indeed, Cocotte was there, and his heart beat freely again. "For without Cocotte," he adds, with a touch of sly malice, "the dear woman would never leave me."

* See Note E—Part III.

Well, she never did leave him, and, so far as we know, she never dreamed of such a thing, great as was her burden. Poor Mathilde! My heart goes out in sympathy to her who was so near the poet, and who is treated with such scant courtesy by the great man's biographers. I believe she suffered more than we know. She was not a literary woman, and she could not leave the world a memoir of that mattress-grave tragedy, as did another woman whose presence at her husband's bedside brought him more comfort than it brought her. She could only retire, at odd times, when her care was not required by the sick man, and talk to her parrot or, perhaps, cry softly to herself.

BUT the end of that long martyrdom was drawing near. Now the poet writes or dictates —for his sight is nearly gone and his paralyzed fingers can not guide the pen: "My body suffers much, but my soul is as placid as a lake, and sometimes the most beautiful sunrises and sunsets are reflected in it." He makes his will, his latest thought anxious for poor Mathilde: "Farewell, thou German fatherland—land of riddles and sorrows; farewell, you kindly French people, whom I have loved so much." Thus he fell asleep, February 17, 1856. The funeral was simple, without any religious ceremony, as the poet had desired. The mourners were Théophile Gautier, Alexandre Dumas the elder, Paul de St. Victor, and Mignet. Dumas wept; Gautier, seeing the great casket and the shrunken corpse, recalled the poet's own lines:

> Do you know why the coffin
> So heavy and wide must be?
> Because in it I laid my love,
> And with it my misery!*

The poet was buried in Montmartre cemetery, according to his wish. I stood beside his tomb in September of last year. Over his grave is a monument surmounted with a bust, bearing the inscription, "Henri Heine." Under the name of the Poet appear the significant words "Frau Heine," and on the sides of the stone are carved Heine's well known verses in German, of which the following is an English version:

> Where shall once the wanderer weary
> Find his resting-place and shrine?
> Under palm trees by the Ganges?
> Under lindens of the Rhine?

* See Note B—Part III.

Shall I somewhere in the desert
   Owe my grave to stranger hands?
Or upon some lonely sea-shore
   Rest at last beneath the sands?

'Tis no matter! God's wide heaven
   Must surround me there as here;
And as death-lamps o'er me swinging,
   Night by night the stars burn clear.

The mother who had brought him into the
world which he filled with his fame, survived
him three years.

XI

THE AWARD

HEINE, in his fine comparison of Goethe and
Schiller, wrote: "Goethe's poems do not
beget deeds as do Schiller's. Deeds are the children of the word, and Goethe's fair words are
childless. That is the curse of all that is the
product of art alone."

Here is a profound truth by virtue of which
Heine himself exercises a more vital influence
than the sovereign of German literature. Heine,
indeed, more potently represents his time, its aspiration, its revolt against tradition and dogma
and all cramping prescription. Hence Matthew
Arnold calls him the paladin of the modern
spirit. The poet truly describes himself as a son
of the Revolution. "Poetry has always been
with me only a sacred plaything," he says. "I
have ever placed but slight value on poetic fame,
and my future repute troubles me not at all. But
if ye will do me honor, lay a sword upon my

coffin lid, for I was a brave soldier in the war of the liberation of humanity."

Doubtless it required more courage and self-sacrifice to live the life that Heine lived—no matter how often it fell below the mark—than to wear a gold chain and be Chancellor at Weimar. It is a great distinction to be a great poet. Add to this the glory of leading and inspiring the onward march of humanity—of suffering also in that supreme cause—and the measure of earthly greatness is filled.

This crowning honor, I believe, can not fairly be refused to the memory of Heinrich Heine.

PART III
ART AND PERSONALITY

I HAVE, as they say, done
nothing in this lovely world.
I have become nothing—nothing but a poet!
—HEINE

I

HEINE THE PATRIOT

GROWING out of the passions and prejudices of the Great War (1914-18) is an attempt by certain writers to paint Heine as utterly un-German in all his ideas, a hater and contemner of everything Germanic—in a word, a Teutono-phobe of the present generation! This of course is to slander the Poet and to do him an injustice which, of all possible injustices, he would have most bitterly resented.

The truth is—and it need not be regarded as paradoxical—that Heine was German to the core; that he deeply loved the German people; that in spite of his mordant satire, he never ceased to long for the Fatherland; and that he suffered a cruel nostalgia of the heart during all the years of his enforced exile in France. "No one who has not lived in exile," he writes, "knows what love of the Fatherland is, with all its sweet fears and yearning sorrows." He refused to become a naturalized citizen of his adopted country, though the step would have made for his comfort and security; and yet he loved France as with a "second heart". Late in life he declared that he asked no prouder inscription for his tomb than these simple words—

"HERE LIES A GERMAN POET."

Heine in truth was intensely, even inordinately sensitive to any reflection upon his German patriotism, attacked as it often was by his enemies. "I detest disloyalty of every kind," he says, "and I could never renounce a German cat or a German dog, however insupportable their fleas and loyalty might be to me. . . . I have not lost a bristle of my Germanity nor a single frill of my German cap, and I have still the vigor to fix on it the black, red and gold cockade!"

Heine has not left us without poetical expression of the deep indwelling love for the Fatherland which made so bitter-sweet his long exile. He who had wittily boasted that his mind was at home on the Seine, his heart on the Rhine, kept nothing back from us in these touching, characteristic verses:

O GERMANY, so far, so dear,
  Thy memory dims mine eye with woe!
This merry France seems sad and drear,
  Her lightsome folk a burden grow.

'Tis reason only, cold and bare,
  In witty Paris that is crowned—
O foolish bells!—O bells of prayer!
  Yonder at home how sweet ye sound!

These men how mannerly! And yet
  Their courteous bow I take amiss:—
The rudeness that of old I met
  Where I was born, was joy to this.

These smiling women! For their lives
  They chatter like a turning mill!
Give me the silent German wives,
  That go to bed demure and still.

Here round and round in frantic chase
  Things whirl as in a dream and move!
There all seems nailed into its place,
  And glides along the ancient groove.

The watchman's horn, I hear it blow:
  Familiar, faint, from far it hails;
The watchman's song, I hear it grow
  And mingle with the nightingale's.

Those were the poet's golden times,
  'Neath Schilda's oaks of shadowy boon;
Where once I wove my tender rhymes
  From violet's breath and light o' moon.

What Heine hated in Germany with a bitter
and truceless hatred was the divine-right, mon-
archical superstition and the hereditary noble
caste supporting it, both of which furnished end-
less provocation to his satirical pen. Also he
detested with a special detestation and a most
intense personal animus the official governing
class, the stupid legislators who had interdicted
his writings (which were not calculated for their
comfort, it must be allowed), that had banned,
proscribed, and kept him an exile. Or it might
be said that Heine loved the *spiritual* Germany,
the Fatherland of hallowed traditions, marvellous legends, august historic memories, while he
hated the *material* Germany given over to the
rule of tyrants, with their satrapies of bigots and
fools. The love and the hatred here allowed
were both natural and necessary to a genius like
Heine; lacking either he would not be the man
we know.

II

THE LYRIST

AND oh! the verses, like the metre of the
French, are insupportable to me—profound
trifles. I can scarcely put up with their odorless
poets. When I consider the so-called *poésie
lyrique,* then I recognize the splendor of German poetry, and then I can plume myself on having won my laurels in that realm. We will not
give up a leaf of them, and the sculptor who has
to adorn our last resting-place with an inscription will not have to expect any contradiction
when he carves there the words:

"Here lies a German poet."
                                        —HEINE

THE poet's vaunt is nobly justified, for Heine
in his peculiar lyrical province is without a
rival in modern letters. His song is that of the
nightingale in pain; no other poet has ever at-
tained such a mastery of the bitter-sweet. When
poetry seemed "done to death" he came with a

fresh manner, which is always the secret of
genius, and by a touch of his wand recreated the
Castalian waters. Perhaps no collection of lyrical verse has ever so poignantly touched the
world's heart as the "Intermezzo". And for another distinction, he is almost the only poet who
constantly interests us—who can be at the same
time both witty and poetical, contradiction in
terms though it seem. With what piercing truth
he said of himself—

> My heart is wise and witty,
> And it bleeds within my breast.

But who can suggest the secret of Heine's lyrical enchantment? I shall wisely say no more but
content myself with quoting two short lyrics of
his which "tell the story" to fit eyes and ears. The
first is, I verily believe, the loveliest poem of
eight lines in the literature of the world.

> A PINE-TREE standeth lonely
> On a far Norland height:
> It slumbereth, while round it
> The snow falls thick and white.

> And of a Palm it dreameth,
> That in a Southern Land

Lonely and silent standeth,
Amid the scorching sand.

The second lyric I would quote, as simple and
inimitably perfect, is indeed known to all lovers
of poetry.

COME, fairest fisher-maiden,
Bring now thy skiff to land;
Come here and sit beside me,
We'll prattle hand in hand.

Oh, lay thy head against my heart,
Have not such fear of me:
Thou trustest day by day thyself
Unto the wild, wild sea.

My heart is like the sea—it hath
Its storm and ebb and flow,
And many wondrous pearls, my dear,
Lurk in its depths below.

He has varied this figure to beautiful purpose,
even in prose:

"I love the sea as my own soul! I often feel as
if the sea must be my soul. And as in the sea
there are hidden water-plants which come to the

surface only at the moment they blossom, and sink again the moment that they fade, so at times there float up from the depths of my soul wondrous flowers of fancy which gleam and bloom and die."

The lyrical pieces of Heine, the heart-songs as they may truly be called, for they fulfil the definition by their deep feeling, without sentimentality, are known the world over:

Like Psaphon's birds speaking their master's
    name
In every language syllabled by fame.

It is doubtful if any other modern poet has been honored to an equal extent by the compliment of translation and the applause of foreign audiences. Even the great Goethe can not sustain the comparison here:—what short poem of his, except the "Mignon" verses from "Wilhelm Meister", has sung itself into so many hearts among all gentle peoples, as have no small number of Heine's lyrics or *lieder?*

And pray, when we speak of modern lyrics, what one of them all is more deservedly famous than "The Lorelei"? In poetical beauty, the lingering spell it casts on the memory, the magical and romantic associations it awakens, the lovely and consummate yet adorably simple art of it, where shall we find the equal of this ballad? Yet a poem that would make a sufficient estate, with title-deeds of immortality, for any man lucky enough to have written it, is but a tiny part of the careless wealth of Heine.

Familiar as this wonder-song of the Rhine must be to every reader of these pages, I can not deny myself the pleasure of reproducing here the admirable version made by the English poet James Thomson.

I KNOW not what evil is coming,
    But my heart feels sad and cold;
A song in my head keeps humming,
    A tale from the times of old.

The air is fresh and it darkles,
    And smoothly flows the Rhine;
The peak of the mountain sparkles
    In the fading sunset-shine.

The loveliest wonderful maiden
    On high is sitting there,
With golden jewels braiden,
    And she combs her golden hair.

With a golden comb sits combing,
  And ever the while sings she
A marvellous song through the gloaming,
  Of magical melody.

It hath caught the boatman, and bound him
  In the spell of a wild sad love;
He sees not the rocks around him,
  He sees only her above.

The waves through the pass keep swinging,
  But boatman or boat is none;
And this with her mighty singing
  The *Lorelei* hath done!

III

THE SATIRIST

THE personal note of Heine's verse is the most piercing in modern poetry; in this respect he has more than equalled the interest which Byron excited. True also is it that Heine is a finer artist, especially of the lyric vein, than the noble English poet. I do not concur in the estimate which ranks Heine as generally a greater poet than Byron, and which certainly would have provoked a protest from the Jupiter of Weimar. Judged by the height and range of his poetical achievement, and allowing for the shortness of his career (he lived twenty years less than Heine), I believe the Englishman is still unmatched. Heine knew his own powers better and made fewer balks; he never seems to have known the amateurishness, the *gaucherie,* with which the other began his literary course, or the culpable inartistry which continued to reproach his maturer years. All this may be allowed, without touching the question of greatness.

As a lyrist, however, Heine decidedly excels; nor has he for the wit, charm and fascination of his prose writings any competitor among the poets. His satirical strain is peculiar to himself and the manner in which he employed it in his finest poetical conceptions, seems altogether without precedent. The art of being both honey and sting with equal effect was his beyond question, and so far at least, he is without a rival. Heine is the poison-flower of poetry, breathing at once the rarest fragrance of life and the evil odor of death. He has armed the lyric with such weapons as were never given to it before—especially the black arrow that flies out of its perfumed heart! And it can not be gainsaid that he has thus furnished literature with one of its most exquisite pleasures. The ease with which it is done marks the supreme art of the performance. For three-quarters of a century imitators in different languages have been trying to ravish his secret and repeat his miracle, and they have not achieved a respectable echo.

Heine's bitter laughter, the irony which, as I have elsewhere said, he wore to protect his heart, is heard and felt most poignantly in the following sonnet, which may also be taken as a sort of *apologia* for his own life. If there be, within similar brief compass, a more powerful poem—rather a more piercing cry than this, or one more painfully arresting, in the range of modern verse, it has not been my good fortune to meet with it.

I ONLY laugh at the invidious grin
    With which the goat-faced herd at me do
      stare;
    I laugh too, at the foxes, who with bare
Gaunt paunches sniff and gape, all hunger-thin.
I laugh too, at the apes that *look* so wise,
    And swell themselves to arbiters of thought;
    I laugh too, at the craven good-for-naught
Who with his poisoned steel in ambush lies.
For when Good Fortune's wreath of Life's best
    flowers
    Is smitten by the hand of adverse Fate,
    And shattered at our feet lies all forlorn;
And when the heart within the breast is torn,
    Torn, broken, cleft in twain and desolate,—
    Why,—shrill, ironic laughter still is ours!

No poet who could be so sweet was ever more bitter; no satirist was ever so truly a poet.
    Gautier remarked (speaking for the French

public) that no poet who has to be read through the medium of a translation *disturbs us so much as Heine*. Not less may be said on behalf of the English-reading public: a wonderful tribute to Heine's compelling genius when we reflect that three-fourths of such a poet is inevitably sacrificed in translation. It has been remarked of some of the best English renderings of Heine's verse that the honey is carried over more easily than the poison—the latter being the peculiar, inalienable property of the poet. If I were to quote only a few of the examples that occur to mind I should soon exceed my space—and this is the difficulty as well as the delight of writing upon Heine, that you are driven to quote or paraphrase him continually (even Gautier has to do it, the most original and felicitous of his commentators). But I want to give the English reader a fair example of the perfect yet poisoned art of Heine—the sort of *theriaca* that he alone of modern poets knows how to compound with deadliest skill and potency. And I can hardly do better than to quote the following verses* of the famous poem "Affrontenberg", which I venture to say is, of its kind, quite unmatched in our literature.

* This translation by Gilbert Cannan does no injustice to the original.

I SEE the ancient castle still—
The turret, and the battled wall,
The stupid folks about the place;
Though years have fled, I see it all.

I still can see the weather-cock
That on the roof went clanking round,
And drew from each a timid glance
Before he dared to make a sound.

None spoke till he had first inquired
In what direction blew the wind,
In case old growling Boreas rude
Might buffet him with breath unkind.

The wise ones simply held their peace,
For in that castle, well they knew,
There was an echo which gave back,
With venomed malice, false for true.

A marble fountain, sphinx-adorned,
Down, midway, in the garden stood.
'Twas always dry, though many a tear
Had fallen by its sealèd flood.

Accursèd garden! Every spot
Some memory of woe has kept;
At every turn my heart was torn,
And everywhere mine eyes have wept.

In truth there grew no single tree
Beneath whose boughs had not been flung
Some insult or abusive speech,
By voice refined, or vulgar tongue.

The toad that listened in the grass
Informed the rat, who, word for word,
Confided to her aunt the snake
The tale the toad had overheard.

The snake rehearsed it to the frog,
And so at once the gossip spread,
And all the filthy fry enjoyed
The insults heaped upon my head.

The garden's roses blossomed fair,
And sweetly lured with odorous breath,
But, victims of some poison strange,
Before their time they drooped to death.

The nightingale, the noble bird,
Who sang the roses in their bloom,
Has perished since, and I believe
The self-same poison wrought his doom.

Accursèd garden! Yes, a curse,
An evil spell upon it lay,
And often with a ghostly fear
I shuddered in the light of day.

I seemed to see a spectre green
That grinned and mocked me, and I heard
A horrid sound of sighs and groans
From out the yew-copse, weirdly stirred.

Down at the garden's further end
A terrace high was built, and, under,
When tides were full, upon the rocks
The North Sea billows broke in thunder.

There, gazing o'er the waters wide,
I dreamed mad dreams of wild unrest;
A fury like the ocean's own
Was foaming, seething in my breast:

A foaming, seething, surging rage,
Vain as the billows', shattered wan
Against the hard and ruthless cliff,
However proudly they came on.

The passing ships I envied sore:
They sailed away to happier lands;
While to that castle I was bound,
A prisoner in accursèd hands.

IV

MOTHER HEINE

HEINE'S love for his mother was one of the strongest tendrils that bound his poet soul to humanity. In spite of their long enforced separation, it is of a piece with his life, breathing from many letters and some exquisite poems, of which "Night Thoughts" is perhaps the best known to English readers. It seems to me quite beyond praise in its expression of natural feeling and homely pathos.

THE thought of Germany at night
Drives slumber from my pillow quite;
My mind recalls the day of parting,
And hot, resistless tears are starting.

The years have come, the years have passed,
Since, Mother dear, I saw thee last;—
Twelve years have gone—gone unreturning—
Yet grows my longing and my yearning.

My yearning and my longing grow,
That mother has bewitched me so;
I think of her as of no other,
May God preserve her, dear old Mother!

The dear old dame, she loves me so!
In trembling lines her letters show,
By signs that cannot be mistaken
How deep her mother's heart is shaken.

Of her I think where'er I stay;
Twelve long, long years have passed away;
Twelve years 'mong strangers have distressed me
Since to her true heart she has pressed me.

Ah, Germany lives evermore,
It is a land sound to the core,
With oaks and lindens firmly rooted;
Whene'er I wish I can salute it.

For Germany I should not care
So much, were not my mother there;
For it no trouble need I borrow,
But she I love may die to-morrow.

Ah, since I left my native land
Death touched with unrelenting hand
My early friends, aye, many perished
Whom in my youth I fondly cherished.

And if I count the shadowy crowd
My heart in anguish throbs aloud;
Could I these mournful figures banish,
I should have rest. Thank God, they vanish.

Thank God! Athwart the window-pane
Serene French daylight shines again;
In comes my wife, like morn in gladness,
And smiles away my German sadness.

Even more delightfully characteristic and
Heinesque are the following witty, humorous
and yet somehow pathetic verses descriptive of
the poet's return to Germany on a visit to his
home and kindred, after many years of exile.
The simplicity and homeliness of this poem need
not blind us to its inimitable art; easy and familiar as it seems, it contains the essence of Heine's
genius.

FROM Hamburg to Homburg we drove in an
hour,
The shades of night were thickening;
The stars of heaven in welcome shone;
The air was soft and quickening.

When I reached my mother's, the dear thing's
joy
Was so great and unexpected

She was almost scared; she clasped her hands
In rapture unaffected.

"My child!   And after thirteen years
Like this again to meet, dear!
You must be hungry; tell me quick,
What will you have to eat, dear?

"I have fish, cold goose, and oranges
The sweetest you ever tasted."
"Then give me the oranges, fish, and goose,
I promise they won't be wasted."

I ate with a will, and my mother was gay,
But alas!   I am no romancer;
She asked me this and she asked me that,
And her questions were hard to answer.

"My darling child, in your foreign home
Are you carefully served and tended?
Does your wife understand how to keep a house?
Are your shirts and stockings mended?"

"Dear little mother, the fish is good,
But fish is a risky diet;
You so easily choke on a bone if you speak;
Just leave me a moment in quiet."

When the excellent fish had been despatched,
The goose was served up duly,
And my mother began her questions again;
It was awkward to answer truly.

"My darling child! In which country, say,
Has life the greater zest now?
You've tried the French and the German both,
And which do you like the best now?"

"Dear mother, this German goose is superb,
But in France a tradition they follow,
When it comes to the stuffing, that's better than
     ours,
And in sauces they beat us hollow."

And after the goose had disappeared
The oranges took their station
Before me in turn, I found them sweet
Beyond all expectation.

But then my mother began again—
When happy you know how one chatters—
She asked me a thousand things, and touched
On painful and personal matters.

"My child! And what are at present your views?
Is your interest still as hearty

V

MATHILDE

HEINE'S love for his Mathilde, given his temperament, was all that she could have asked, and to us it seems the more beautiful and pathetic from the fact that he appears to have regarded her as a child. Their union, at first a mere accident of passion, ended in a true marriage that, in the last years, was the one source of consolation to the stricken poet. His letters to her, during his brief absences from her side, overflow with tenderness, and there are not wanting paternal admonitions, shrewd and pointed. Let us peep into a few of the Mathilde-letters—we shall not find a different Heine there.

From Bremen—1843:

Dear Treasure! My heart is full of care—I have left my poor lamb in Paris where there are many wolves. I am the poor half of a cock. I have already spent more than a Hundred Dollars. Adieu! I embrace you.

* * * * *

From Hamburg—1843:

Beautiful Treasure: Karl Heine laughs at my jealousy, and is surprised that I was able to resolve to leave you in Paris. You are my poor beloved wife, and I hope that you are well-behaved and reasonable.

*   *   *   *   *

I pray you not to show yourself too much in public. . . . I hope you will not receive the chief of fools in your house; believe me, you have friends and former friends, women who ask nothing better than to compromise you in my sight.

*   *   *   *   *

I am thinking only of you, my dear Nanette. It was a great resolve to leave you all alone in Paris, that fearful abyss! Do not forget that my eyes are always upon you. I know everything that you do, and what I don't know now I shall learn later on.

*   *   *   *   *

You are always in my thoughts, and I cannot be at ease. Indefinite and melancholy fears torture me day and night. You are the only joy of my life—don't make me unhappy. I hope you will be richly rewarded for your present boredom. I will do everything possible to indemnify you for it. Adieu, my angel, my dearest, my poor child, my good wife!

* * * * *

I am ill and bored, for I think always of you. I am almost mad when my thoughts turn towards Chaillôt. What is my wife, the craziest of the crazy, doing now? It was madness of me not to bring you with me here. For God's sake, do nothing which might make me angry when I return. Keep as quiet as possible in your little nest; work, study, be bored virtuously, spin wool like the honest Lucretia, whom you saw at the Odéon.

* * * * *

No news of you for such a long time! My God! I assure you, it is terrible. . . . I shall return straight to Paris, without stopping anywhere, so that I may see you again in a fortnight, my treasure. Meanwhile be calm, industrious and prudent.

* * * * *

The main thing is that I am on my way (home), that I am well, and that I love you with all my heart, and that I shall probably embrace you on Saturday. I am tormented with anxiety

about you.   To be so long without news of you—
Oh God, how terrible! I am angry with you,
too, and when I arrive I shall only give you five
hundred kisses instead of a thousand.

* * * * *

From Hamburg—1844:
I have been worried to death since you left.
. . . Three days since I saw you—these days
have vanished like shadows. . . . Write to me
soon and much—you need not be afraid of me.
Let me know if you got through all right . . .
and if I may be easy about you. Keep quiet in
your nest until I return.

* * * * *

I am three hundred hours away from you; in
a word, I am not happy, I await impatiently letters from you. I charged you to write to me at
least twice a week, for I am not easy about you.
I lose my head, and yet more than ever there is
need of my poor head, for the horizon is dark-
ened and my affairs are in confusion. . . . I
have no need to bid you be prudent in everything
that you do.

* * * * *

I am very busy at present, and as I am only
writing and speaking German, I find it a little

difficult to write in French. That may explain
to you why I do not write to you as often and as
long letters as I would like to do; for I always
think of you, and I have a thousand things to say
to you. The most important thing that I have
to say is, that *I love you to distraction, my dear
wife!*

*   *   *   *   *

I do pray you not to leave me without letters,
but to write me much and as often as possible.
Do not forget that I only live for you, and if you
are not happy at present, do not be uneasy—the
future is ours.

I add a few allusions to Mathilde dating from
the first years of their connection.

To August Lewald (April, 1835):

How am I to excuse my silence? . . . I was
up to my neck in a love-affair, from which I have
not yet extricated myself. Since October nothing has been of the least importance to me that
has not been connected with this affair. I have
neglected everything, seen no one, and at best a
sigh has escaped me when I thought of my
friends. . . . Have you read the Song of Songs
which is the Song of Solomon? Well, read it

again, and you will find in it all I could tell you to-day.

To Julius Campe (1835):

I, poor fool, thought that the time of passion was gone for me—that I could never again be dropped into the angry whirlpool of humanity, that like the immortal Gods, I was at peace, serenity and moderation—and lo! I raged again like a man, like a young man.

To August Lewald (1836):

My Mathilde is sitting by my side in front of a great fireplace, working at my new shirts. . . . I have been living very pleasantly in Paris lately, and Mathilde has brightened life for me with the consistent inconsistency of her whims—I think only occasionally of poisoning or asphyxiating myself! . . .

Herr —— said so much to her in praise of my writings that she had no rest until I got the French edition of the Travel Pictures for her. But scarcely had she read a page of it than she grew pale as death, trembled in all her limbs, and begged me for God's sake to put the book away. She had chanced on a love passage, and being jealous, she would like me never to have paid homage to any other before her dominion began. I had to promise her that henceforth I would not make love to any ideal woman in my books.

To the same (1837):

You will have received through Herr —— the pretty tapestry which Mathilde worked for you; she showed by this tedious piece of labor that she was very industrious and therefore faithful to me in my absence. . . . We are both very happy living together; that is, I do not have a moment's peace day or night.

To the same (1837):

Mathilde has insisted this year on travelling with me instead of enjoying the summer at home in the village with her mother. But her companionship is difficult because of the dear creature's wildness, which is a constant source of trouble to me.

To J. H. Detwold (1837):

My passion for Mathilde grows more chronic every day; she is well, and troubles me more in my dreams than in reality. . . . I enjoy in full draughts the sorrow of possession—I was lately in her village and experienced the most incredible idyll. Her mother gave me Mathilde's first little chemise, and this sad little piece of linen is before me as I write.

To August Lewald (1840):

Mathilde has become a good housewife, in spite of her crazy temper, and our domestic life is as moral as the best in Krähwinkel.*

To Maximilian Heine, his brother (1843):

My wife is a good, frank, merry child, capricious as only a Frenchwoman can be, and she does not suffer me to fall into melancholy German dreams. For eight years I have loved her with a tenderness and passion incredible.

HEINE'S relation to Mathilde is sufficiently disclosed in the letters † from which these extracts are made; and it is of a sort that inclines the world to view him with more kindness. She was for him the Beloved Woman; she satisfied his heart without making appeal on other grounds. Indeed, she cared nothing for and understood little about his poetic fame; and Heine tells someone in his letters that she refused to read his poems in French. However, it has been demonstrated in no lack of instances—even the celebrated instance of Goethe—that love can exist without literary sympathies on the part of the woman. Surely it did in this romance of

* A small village near Düsseldorf.
† Heinrich Heine's Memoirs, edited by Gustav Karpeles, English translation by Gilbert Cannan.

Heine and Mathilde. The passion between them lasted from youth to age, with a fervor and constancy very unusual in such connections. Heine's Germanic tenderness has thrown about it something of the ineffable charm of the Blue Flower.

Two poems written on the eve of his death illustrate the poet's characteristic moods of feeling toward his Mathilde. The first I shall quote is of the rarest beauty and tenderness, depicting his great love and anxious concern for the faithful, helpless creature he must soon leave behind to the world's cold defence and colder charity.

O LITTLE lamb, I was assigned
To be thy shepherd true and kind;
And mid this barren world and rude
To shelter thee as best I could.
I gave thee of my bread thy fill,
I brought thee water from the rill;
And through the raging winter storm
Safe in my bosom kept thee warm.

I held thee close in fond embrace;
And when the cold rain fell apace,
When through the gorge the torrents poured,
And wolves and floods in concert roared,
Thou didst not tremble then, nor fear,
E'en when the lightning's mighty spear

Cleft the tall pine—upon my breast
Still thou didst sleep and calmly rest.

My arm grows weak, and faint my heart,
Pale Death creeps near. The shepherd's part
Is now played out, the game is o'er.
O God, then in Thy hands once more
I lay the crook, and do Thou keep
My little lamb, when I to sleep
Am laid. Oh, guard her day by day
From every harm: and shield, I pray,
Her fleece from storms that may bring pain,
And from the miry swamps that stain.
Beneath her feet, in field and wood,
Let greenest pastures spring for food;
And let her calmly sleep and rest,
As once she slept upon my breast.

Again the playful mockery—the smile that
was Heine even to the last—is seen and heard in
the gently ironic verses addressed to Mathilde,
which he calls "The Anniversary".

THEY will sing for me no masses,
Not a *kaddisch* will be said
In devout commemoration
Of the day my spirit fled.

But I shall not be forgotten;
If the weather is serene,
Frau Matilda may go walking
On Montmartre with Pauline.

And some immortelles she'll carry,
On my grave the wreath she'll set,
And she'll sigh, *"Pauvre homme!"* and sadly
Drop a tear of soft regret.

And alas! too high in Heaven
I shall be to give my sweet
Even a chair to sit and rest on,
Though she sway with weary feet.

Listen, plump and pretty darling:
Home afoot you must not go;
You will see outside the gateway
Hackney carriages arow.

VI

HEINE AND RELIGION

A GREAT deal has been put forth by Heine's friends and foes alike on the subject of his religious belief or unbelief, and, as it seems to me, with small profit or edification. After the Heine-lovers and the Heine-haters have had their voluminous say, one has still to ask oneself the pertinent question—"What was Heine's religion?"

But ere we attempt to suggest an answer to the query, let it be noted, *imprimis,* that the poet is himself mainly responsible for the confusion amongst his apologists and denunciators. Each and all, they are able to make a case out of his writings, public and private—an *ex parte* case, to be sure—and still a candid reader may well feel that the truth has eluded them. For this we can only blame the extraordinary mental and spiritual elasticity of Heine—not his love of mockery, his inherent irreverence or ungodliness, as his censors would put it. Indeed, if Heine were the out-and-out mocker and desecrator that he has been painted, it would not be worth while to waste a page under the above heading. He has written abundantly both prose and verse which give the lie to such a character.

But there is undeniably a great difficulty in getting at the truth and doing him the measure of justice to which a writer of his high rank is entitled. And this difficulty arises from his possession of the most versatile and contradictory sympathies as regards religion—a condition, be it said, which offers certain advantages to the poet, but is fatal to the sectary or theologue.

Heine at times praised and admired all the Creeds—even, though very rarely, the Creed of Infidelity—and then again at times mocked them all and branded them with the light iron of satire. He was born a Jew and, as we shall see, he reverted in the end to his first belief in a Personal God—the God of Israel. But yet he condemned the Jews as "an accursed race who came from Egypt, the land of crocodiles and priestcraft, and brought with them, besides certain skin diseases and the vessels of gold and silver that they stole, a so-called positive religion and a so-called church".

This is giving the sword to the hilt; the satire of Heine has yielded nothing more deadly. And yet a man might write so and still believe in God.

He might even sketch this poetic picture of the Man-God and his Mission (by the way, no florid Chateaubriand, no Christian pietistic writer whatever, has come anywhere near it):

—Then he poured wine to all the other gods from left to right, ladling the sweet nectar from the bowl, and laughter unquenchable arose amid the blessed gods to see Hephaistos bustling through the palace. So they feasted all day till the setting of the sun; nor was their soul aught stinted of the fair banquet, nor of the beauteous lyre that Apollo held, and the Muses singing alternately with their sweet voices—   —The Iliad.

When suddenly a pale, breathless, blood-stained Jew entered, bearing a crown of thorns on his head, and on his shoulder a great cross of wood. And as he threw this cross upon the gods' great banquet table, the golden goblets were shaken, the gods were stricken dumb, they grew pale and ever paler till at last they faded away into vapor.

This is mere literature, perhaps—a purple patch, if you will; but it could not have been written by a coarse mocker and hater of religion.

Heine angrily repudiated this character which his enemies sought to fasten upon him, and declared that those who called him a second Voltaire did him too much honor. "I do not hate the altar," he said, "but I hate those serpents which lurk under the ruined stones of old altars." Again, he declared himself a friend of the State and of Religion, but "I hate that abortion which is called State-Religion—that object of derision born from the concubinage of temporal and spiritual power".

His hatred of State-Religion is intelligible enough, remembering what he had to suffer from official intolerance in Germany. "Were there no such State-Religions," he affirms, "no privileges pertaining to a dogma and a cult, Germany would be united and strong, her sons would be great and free."

Again he asserts: "I honor the inner holiness of each religion. . . . If I have no special veneration for anthropomorphism, yet I believe in the omnipotence of God."

These quotations I have purposely made from writings of his prime, when his genius and intellectual activity were at flood-tide. Surely they afford small warrant for the judgment that writes him down as an Atheist and a flouter of all things sacred.

I have spoken of his versatile sympathies in

regard to different religions, which sprang no doubt in part from his great culture, but I believe mainly from the richness of his artistic endowment. Indeed, as proving his poetic sympathy with religious forms and beliefs otherwise alien to him, I may quote here his words regarding the Roman Catholic Church, written toward the end of his life. Treating of a rumor that he had turned Catholic (which arose from his having married Mathilde according to the Catholic rite *) Heine says:

"I can not be accused of fanatical hostility toward the Roman Catholic Church, for I always lacked the narrow-mindedness which is necessary for such animosity. I am too well acquainted with my own spiritual stature not to know that I could not do much harm to a colossus like St. Peter's by a crazy assault. . . . As a thinker and

---

* In regard to his marriage, after admitting that it had been performed in a Jesuit Church (St. Sulpice) Heine says in his Confessions: "I had my marriage solemnized there following the civil ceremony, because my wife, being of a Catholic family, believed that she would not be properly married, in the sight of God, without such a ceremony. Unbelief is, besides, very dangerous in marriage; however free-thinking I may have been, there could never be spoken in my house one frivolous word."

He has written elsewhere: "Beautiful women without any religion are like flowers without scent."

metaphysician I had even to pay my tribute of
admiration to the consistency of the Roman Catholic dogma; and I can pride myself on never
having fought either dogma or rites with wit and
satire; I have been shown too much honor and
dishonor in being called an intellectual kinsman
of Voltaire. I have always been a poet, and
therefore the poetry which flowers and glows in
the symbolism of the Catholic dogma and worship, has been more profoundly revealed to me
than to other people, and in my youth I was not
infrequently overwhelmed by the infinite sweetness, the mysterious and holy sentimentality, and
the strange death-longing of that poetry. Often
I was filled with enthusiasm for the blessed
Queen of Heaven. I turned into stately rhymes
the legends of her grace and goodness, and my
first collected poems contain traces of that beautiful Madonna-period, which I expunged with
such absurd care in later collections."

CERTAIN it is that literature has been greatly
enriched by Heine's versatile, even contrasted,
moods in regard to religion.

However these moods may have varied during
his years of health and full activity, he seems not
to have changed his practice—which was to have

the least possible to do with churches and church-
men. He parted with Lutheranism immediately
upon leaving the church where he had been bap-
tized as a convert, and he left his newly taken
Christian names behind him.*

But now we come to the story of the last years
and the formal recantation of his religious here-
sies. It is not the least interesting and extraordinary phase of an unexampled career. The so-
called "death-bed repentance" of Heine has been
greatly exaggerated by those who regarded him
as an arch-mocker and sinner against light, ex-
piating his offences under a signal act of Divine
chastisement. The effect of such a moral lesson,
even when in the fullest sense edifying, is rather
doubtful in our modern eyes. After all, the
man's life alone is conclusive; his death changes
nothing. Napoleon teaching the Catechism at
St. Helena does not approximate him to St. Fran-
cis of Assisi. On the other hand, Voltaire's alleged recantation of infidelity has not in the
slightest degree altered his terrible rôle as the
Hammer of Christianity. Nor have Heine's late

* This is not strictly correct. At his Lutheran baptism he
took the names of Christian Johann Heinrich. His parents
had named him *Harry,* not Heinrich, after an English friend
of his father. The change was a fortunate one, and so much
credit at least should be allowed to his "conversion".

concessions to the religious spirit and the moral change in him wrought by his mattress-grave reflections, much availed to change the purport of his life and work. It is true the world was startled to hear from *Eulenspiegel* a strain that seemed to belong to the Man of Uz; but the plagiarism was never very convincing—and *Eulenspiegel* had the last word.

But lest we ourselves sin against grace, it is beyond doubt that the terrible afflictions of Heine's last years moved him to sober thought and a sensible revision of his attitude toward the Eternal Truths. In all apparent earnestness he declares: "I owe the resurrection of my religious feeling to that holy book, the Bible; and it was for me as much a source of health as an occasion for pious admiration. Strange that, after having passed all my life in gliding about the dancing floors of philosophy and abandoning myself to all the orgies of intellect, and dallying with systems that never satisfied me—I have suddenly taken my stand on the Bible and knelt in devotion beside my black brother, Uncle Tom!"

To Julius Campe, his publisher, he writes in 1850—six years before the end:

"I have not become a hypocrite, but I will not play tricks with God; as I deal honestly with men, so will I with God also, and in everything that was produced in my earlier period of blasphemy I have plucked out the fairest poisoned flowers with a firm hand, and in my physical blindness I have doubtless thrown many an innocent flower that grew side by side with them, into the fire."

In the same year he wrote (preface to the "Romancero"):

"Yes, I have made my peace with the Creator, to the great distress of my enlightened friends, who reproached me with this backsliding into the old superstitions, as they preferred to call my return to God! I was overcome by divine home-sickness, and was driven by it through woods and valleys, over the dizziest mountain paths of dialectics. On my way I found the God of the Pantheists, but I had no use for him, because he is not really a God—for the Pantheists are only Atheists ashamed. . . . But I must expressly contradict the rumor that my retrogression led me to the steps of any Church or to its bosom. . . . I have forsworn nothing—not even my old Pagan gods, from whom I have indeed turned, though we parted in love and friendship."

To Campe in 1851 he writes with painful significance:

"I suffer very, very much and endure the pangs of Prometheus, through the rancor of the gods who have a grudge against me because I have given men a few night-lights and farthing dips. I say 'the gods,' because I wish to say nothing about *the* God. I know *his* Vultures now, and have every respect for them."

Half martyr, half mocker Heine remained even unto the end, and the cynical note constantly recurs to spoil what would have been otherwise no doubt a tremendously edifying "conversion". Good Christians will see in all this a visible contest between the poet's Good Angel and the Dark Enemy of mankind; Heine himself accounted for it characteristically enough in one of his imperfectly sanctified moods:

"A religious reaction has set in upon me for some time. God knows whether the morphine or the poultices have anything to do with it. I believe again in a personal God: to this we come when we are sick, sick to death and broken down. If the German people accept the King of Prussia in their need, why should not I accept a personal God? When health is used up, money used up also, and sound human senses destroyed,

Christianity begins. . . . For the sick man it is a very good religion."

Heine's declaration of religious belief, in his Will, is of capital interest, because (as it seems to the present writer) of its essential consistency, and also because of its deliberate character. It was not a hurried, death-bed avowal, as some have ignorantly supposed, but, on the contrary, a long-meditated, careful expression of the poet's thought and purpose. The dates put this beyond question. Heine's Will was attested in November, 1851; his death occurred in February, 1856.

Respecting religion he declares as follows in the Will:

"Although I belong to the Lutheran Confession by the act of baptism, I do not desire that the ministers of that church should be invited to my burial; and I object to any other sort of priest officiating at my funeral. This objection does not spring from any kind of free-thinking prejudice. For the last four years I have renounced all pride of philosophy and returned to religious ideas and feelings. I die in faith in one God, the eternal Creator of the World, whose pity I beseech for my immortal soul. I regret having sometimes spoken of sacred things without due reverence in my writings, but I was led astray more by the spirit of the time than by my own inclination. If I have unwittingly offended against good morals and the morality which is the true essence of all monotheistic doctrines of faith, I do ask pardon of God and man."

ALL these confessions and declarations were I think mainly uncalled for and sprang from the conditions of Heine's terrible disease. Far greater sinners in kind than he have lived out man's allotted term and passed to their account without exemplary agonies. Heine's extreme self-consciousness, working with his spinal complaint, played him a sad trick; the pathologic element in these tackings and veerings of conscience, this half-hearted repudiation of self, seems only too obvious. Behind it all, too, one detects the exaggerated egoism of the dying. What sick man does not view himself as the most important person in the world?—and here was one who had long occupied an intellectual throne!

A quicker or a kindlier death, and perhaps we should have had none of the edifying recantations referred to. And one can't help suspecting that in the event of a complete recovery,

Heine would have ironically explained them away!

Finally, the poet deceived himself in his fever-bred fears of the old terrible Hebrew God without pity or humor; and he exaggerated the measure of his offending. Heine was not of the Titans who storm Heaven and aim their blows at the Thunder-bearer himself; and who, beaten back, recoil upon their unconquerable pride.

I doubt if his writings have ever made a single infidel or caused any one to mock at the true sources of the religious sentiment. The clergy in our time have lost one of their privileges: because a man is witty they dare no longer impeach him as an enemy of God!

Charity is the most precious virtue of the Christian dispensation, and it is one which the world still receives and practises with reluctance: as we see from the memorable example of Heinrich Heine.

In the fulness of intellectual power Heine assumed various masks, at the caprice of his wonderful fantastic genius, and he has even peeped at us from behind the vizor of *Mephistopheles.* But he never entirely forgot that he was *a poet by the grace of God;* and the sum of his work proves him not unworthy of that Divine title.

VII

GERMAN PHILOSOPHERS

IN his "Confessions" Heine relates how he experienced a change of heart in regard to the Hegelian philosophy, which he had intended to set forth at length in a new edition of his book on Germany. This change of heart was induced, he says, by a growing repugnance to Atheism and Godlessness, to which Hegel's philosophy strongly inclined. Accordingly, he tells us that after having occupied himself during two years with this arid subject—"I was no longer happy in my work on the Hegelian philosophy". And he continues:

"I saw clearly that it would not be good either for the public or the author to publish it. I saw that the thinnest soup of Christian charity must be more life-giving for famishing humanity than the grey cobweb mess of the Hegelian dialectics —yes, I will confess everything; I was filled at once with great fear of the everlasting fire. It is superstition, but I was afraid—and on a quiet winter's evening when a good fire was burning in my chimney, I made use of the opportunity and threw my manuscript on the Hegelian philosophy into the glowing coals; the burning pages flew up the chimney with a strange crackling.

"Thank God, I was rid of them! Oh, if I could only destroy everything that I have published about German philosophy in the same way!"

This, however, would have been too great a pity and a deodand costly beyond reason or proportion. Heine's account of German philosophy, a brilliant *précis* sparkling with humor and persiflage, is, nevertheless, as sane as it is brilliant and contains some of his most original and suggestive thought. Further, it is an astonishing proof of his breadth of mind and the amplitude of his learning, which he bore without pedantry. Indeed, the German philosophers might all be spared, *i. e.,* their voluminous works, but not the book which Heine wrote upon them. His unfailing wit and fertility of thought enliven the work throughout, and it is still eminently readable, in spite of the present repugnance of the world-at-large toward German philosophy—or indeed anything "made in Germany".

I have noted the sprightliness of this book of Heine's dealing with so dry a theme as Teuton metaphysics, and I may quote in point his reference to Jacob Boehme, a mystical cobbler of the seventeenth century, who had a considerable following in his time, and who is not yet entirely forgotten. Heine admits that his writings were highly praised by his contemporaries, and then adds: "But I could never make up my mind to read him—I do not like to be made a fool of!"

I suspect this to be the attitude of many people toward works of the same character—they do not wish to be guilty of a foolishness. And next to contemplating one's navel in the Buddhistic fashion, thinking about thought, the philosophic fashion of Germany, is surely as unwise and jejune an occupation as one could desire.

It is the more useless that understanding of the German philosophers—not to go back of Kant—is seldom achieved by the brightest and most persevering minds. It is clear that Heine, with all his cleverness and an undoubted relish for these profound studies, was not so much at home in them as he pretended to be. Often in the midst of a charming discourse, penetrated with the rarest genius and fancy, the lecturer breaks off suddenly, and then hurries on to talk about something else, like a *cicerone* who has forgotten his lines. Ah! who would not prefer the poet's rippling chatter to all the dusty philosophies in his beloved Germania? Be sure that many people will continue to read there, in the poet's golden book, the names of Wolff, Kant, Fichte, Schiller, Hegel, *et al.,* without ever seeking to know more of them and their works.

There is an excellent reason why most people are repelled from reading German philosophy. A little story concerning the great Hegel, for which Herr Heinrich Heine, Doctor of Laws, is responsible, explains it.

When that famous philosopher lay on his death-bed, he remarked sadly: "Only one man has ever understood me." Then after a pause added, "And *he* did not understand me either!"

Concerning the same Hegel, whom Heine grotesquely pictures as "a brood hen sitting on the eggs of Atheism", the poet relates a more famous anecdote in his "Confessions".

"One beautiful starlit night, Hegel stood with me at an open window. I, being then a young man of twenty-two, and having just eaten well and drunk my coffee, spoke with enthusiasm of the stars, and called them the abodes of the blest. But the master muttered to himself, 'The stars! Hm! hm! The stars are only a brilliant eruption on the firmament.' 'What!' cried I, 'then is there no blissful spot above, where virtue is rewarded after death?' But he, glaring at me with his pale eyes, remarked, sneeringly, 'So you want a bonus because you have supported your sick mother and refrained from poisoning your brother?' "

POOR German philosophers! Antics of thought! Some amongst you believed that you had ended the worship of Christ and destroyed the charming Christian Paradise so attractive to children, and to which only the Jews could possibly object. But like the Great Martyr himself, you were not understood, and your words produced nothing save a foolish wonder. You thought to take the Eternal God out of his Heaven as a clocksmith might take down the town clock from the market place, and for a brief time the little German world gaped around you with a fearful expectancy. But nothing happened of any importance, and the gapers went about their business presently, and the long grass waves above your graves—undoubtedly the very species of vegetation that whispered the secret of Midas!

This also was the later persuasion of Heine himself, for twenty years after he had published his work on German philosophy and religion, we find him saying, in a preface to the definitive edition:

"I here candidly confess that everything in this book which relates to the great question of God, is as false as it is foolish. And just as irrational and false is the assertion that Deism was theoretically doomed and must for the future drag out a feeble life in the world of mere shams. No, it is not true that the critic of reason . . . has put an end to the existence of God Himself! For Deism lives—lives its most lively life; it is not dead, and least of all, has it been killed by the last German philosophy. This cobweb Berlin dialectic cannot entice a dog out of the kitchen, or kill a cat, much less a God!"

VIII

ENGLISH IMPRESSIONS

IN many respects John Bull was Heine's life-
long *bête noire,* but this prejudice did not
serve to blind his political vision, which was
marvellously keen, while his deductions were
original and just.   He esteemed the English in
their world-conquering rôle as the due successors
of the ancient Romans—an observation which has
even more weight to-day than when it was first
uttered.   And he never scanted his appreciation
of the great poets* and true intellectual leaders
of the race.

The result of Heine's one and only visit to
England was a book called "English Fragments", published in his twenty-sixth year, which
may still be read with rare interest and pleasure.

Heine makes no pretence to conceal his aver-

* "Byron was the only man," he says, "to whom I felt
myself related, and we may well have a good deal of resemblance in many things."

sion from the English people, whether real or assumed, and the book is well poisoned with observations and reflections in his most satirical vein. He was at the height of his Napoleonic fever, and he could not forgive the conquerors of his Idol. In later years he was wont to smile at his anti-British rabies, although it can not be said that he ever made any formal recantation or apology.

It must, however, be set down to his credit that he was a great admirer of Shakespeare, possessed with an understanding of his genius such as very few foreigners (or for that matter, native English) have ever displayed. Indeed, he does not scruple to claim in his "Shakespeare's Maidens and Women" that the Germans have comprehended Shakespeare better than the English, and he praises Lessing for having "borne the first and heaviest stone for a temple to the greatest of all poets"; while he gives due credit to Schlegel, Wieland, Tieck and other Teutonic poets and scholars who have helped to interpret Shakespeare to the mind of Germany and given him the kingship in the German theatre which he still holds, even better than his native sovereignty.

Heine's book on the women of Shakespeare

concludes with a fantasy on the Shakespearian Comedy—a piece of poetical imagination brilliant as a cascade of fireworks, and I venture to hold, as exquisite a tribute as the Muse of Shakespeare has ever inspired. This book, though unlabored and written mainly as letterpress for a volume of engravings, is a first-rate production of Heine's genius and, besides, in great part ranks as one of the most valuable and suggestive essays on Shakespeare ever written. It is a maturer work than "English Fragments", and appeared a dozen years later (1839); but the author's malice has not much softened in the interval, as we may judge from these few introductory sentences:

"I know a good Hamburg Christian who can never reconcile himself to the fact that our Lord and Saviour was by birth a Jew. A deep dissatisfaction seizes him when he must admit to himself that the Man who, as the pattern of perfection, deserves the highest honor, was still of kin to those shuffling, long-nosed fellows who go running about the streets selling old clothes, whom he so utterly despises, and who are even more desperately detestable when they—like himself—apply themselves to the wholesale business of spices and dye-stuffs, and encroach upon his interests. . . . As Jesus Christ is to this excellent son of Hammonia, so is Shakespeare to me. It takes the heart out of me when I remember that he is an Englishman and belongs to the most repulsive race which God in his wrath ever created."

To return to the "English Fragments". Touched with exaggeration and undue animus as undoubtedly is a great part of these impressions, the book which contains them is still, as I have said, delightfully readable—one of the Heine things that no lover of his talent can afford to miss.

How deep is our passion for tracing the footsteps of genius and seeing all things through its eyes! I have turned over countless descriptions of London and London bridge, but I remember only Heine's. Similarly, of the many accounts of Edmund Kean's acting that I have read, all have faded save the brilliant word-picture of Heine.

Moreover, it can not be denied that Heine's perception of national character was both shrewd and wise, even in his youth; and at no period of his life did he lack what may be called political vision. So his little book on England can still be read with profit, making due deductions on the score of the writer's *parti pris* and his wicked disposition to poke fun at the lordly Britisher. The reason for this is, of course, mainly that Heine was a genius, and as such his views have a great interest for us, quite aside from the question of their fairness or wrong-headedness.

As a sample of Heine's "fun" *re* the English-man, the following may be quoted without breaking any friendships:

"When I was introduced to the Governor of Heligoland, the wooden Englishman stood mo-tionless before me for a few minutes without speaking a word, and involuntarily the idea came into my mind to look at him from behind, to see if somebody had forgotten to wind him up. In fact, out of every Englishman there is engen-dered a certain gas, the carbonic gas of *ennui*. And this I have observed, not only in England where the air is heavy with it, but in Southern countries where the travelling Englishman goes about in isolation, and the grey aureole of *ennui* which surrounds his head is sharply visible in the blue air."

The ply seems to have been very strongly taken, for even as late as 1842 Heine writes, after a four-weeks' visit at Boulogne-sur-mer, which he calls an English town ("You see nothing but English people there, and from morning to night hear nothing but English.")—

"It is surely terribly unjust to condemn a whole people. And with regard to the English I am like to forget, in viewing the mass of them, the many fine and noble men who are distinguished by their intellect and love of liberty. . . . But the run of them, the stockish English—God forgive me—do offend me to my inmost soul, and sometimes I cannot regard them as my fellowmen, but as lamentable automatic machines whose mainspring is egoism. I do confess that I am not altogether impartial when I speak of the English and my aversion from them; my condemnation originates perhaps in my anxiety for the peace and happiness of my German Fatherland. Since I have learned what base calculations prevail in politics, these English have filled me with horrible and unbounded fears."

Remembering that Heine was a true *vates, i. e.,* a soothsayer as well as a poet, these just quoted words of his may be regarded in the light of a prophecy fulfilled.

On account of the provocative writings above referred to, Heine was long *persona non grata* to the English literary world. (Carlyle could find no handsomer epithet for him than "that blackguard".) Within recent years, however, his fame has prospered in England, and the old attainder against him has been suffered to lapse. All honor due to his rank as a world-classic has been accorded him and his books have been translated for English readers in a manner worthy of their merit. Great poets and scholars have vied in the task of interpreting his elusive and enigmatic genius. Even the British Philistine has given him a surly nod of recognition; and it must be allowed that the stiff-necked English can render full measure of justice to an enemy—when he is well and surely dead!

Noting the old hostility toward Heine in England as called forth by the work referred to, the late William Sharp, author of a most sympathetic and eloquent life of the poet*, has these eminently just remarks:

"One would think that Heine's satirical shafts against Frenchmen and Germans were mere unadorned truths, whereas anything spoken against England must of necessity be due to prejudice or envy! Or again, are we not nationally apt, to say the least of it, to be oblivious to the fact that

* And of a rarer, more precious fame as the author of the Fiona Macleod poems.

we have ourselves long mercilessly ridiculed foreigners of all races? As some anonymous writer upon Heine once remarked, 'His ridicule of English awkwardness is as merciless as—English ridicule of German awkwardness'."

Mr. Sharp, while holding Heine's admiration of Napoleon to be excessive, and his hatred of England to some extent crude and incomprehensive, allows that "everywhere save in England his views concerning the relative greatness of Wellington and Napoleon are more or less thoroughly endorsed".

This candid Englishman scores his fellow-countrymen for their condemnation of Heine's religious apostasy in language too strong for me to quote, and affirms that nine-tenths of them would have done the same thing, "had they been German Jews in the present (Nineteenth) century".

IX

THE FRANKFORT AFFAIR

THERE can be no mistake about Heine's high
spirit and physical courage—he possessed
both in a degree that has been with little fairness
called "un-Jewish". In one of his letters to
Moser dated September, 1828, he relates a suggestive incident:

"At Genoa a rascal swore by the Madonna to
stab me. The police told me that such people
kept their word as a matter of conscience, and
advised me to leave the place immediately—but
I stayed for six days, and continued my usual
walks by night along the sea-shore."

Heine bore himself with marked bravery in
the quarrel with one Solomon Straus of Frankfort, which began with slander on both sides, and
ended in a duel. It must be allowed that Straus
had excellent provocation, Heine having grossly
aspersed his wife (Madame Wohl) in his malignant memoir of Börne. Straus was one of a

clique of Jews at Frankfort who had continued Börne's quarrel and pursued the poet even in Paris, after the manners of their kind. Heine's letters show how deeply he felt this ignoble persecution, but they do not relieve him of the odium which brought Herr Straus into the field.

In strict truth, the Poet's attack upon Madame Wohl was the most discreditable act of his life, and the whole book so far as it relates to Börne, his former friend and compatriot, must be deemed altogether unworthy of him. It is true that Heine later made some amends by suppressing a great part of the book, and he offered to apologize to Madame Wohl; but the memory of the double offence remains to stain his shield.

Culpable as he might be in provoking the quarrel, Heine acted like a man of courage throughout the affair, and though Straus was the challenger, the greater eagerness seemed to be on the side of the challenged. The duel was with pistols, and Heine proved that he fought better with the pen. He was slightly wounded in the hip, while the Frankforter went scatheless. This was the Poet's only "affair of honor."

Scarcely anything in Heine's life served to prejudice him more in the eyes of his compatriots —especially the Jews, who had never forgiven the apostasy—than this Börne-Madame Wohl passage. The poet suffered intensely as a result of this quarrel, which was waged with all the bitterness of a family feud; and he never was able to forget the odium of it. In a letter to Lewald written shortly after the duel, the following striking passage occurs:

"My life was beautiful! I had become the favorite poet of Germany, and I was even crowned like a German Emperor at Frankfort. Girls clad in white strewed flowers before me. Oh, it was beautiful! Why, then, had I to make my way home through the Jewish Quarter, which, as you perhaps know, is not far from the Römer! When I marched through it on my triumphal way, an angry woman crossed my path and threatened me, as though she wished to prophesy evil for me. I stopped, fell back a pace, and my wreath—my splendid wreath, fell into the mire of the gutter. Woe is me! a dreadful smell clings to my laurels—a smell which I can not remove. What a pity for my lovely, lovely wreath!"

X

THE BURIED MEMOIRS

AMONG the lost or suppressed works of genius none has offered a more tantalizing bait to literary curiosity than Heine's Memoirs of his own life, frequently alluded to in his private letters.

As Heinrich Heine wrote very much and always charmingly about himself, the acute reader will not suppose that I am overlooking the pages of Autobiography entitled "Confessions", which were dictated about a year before his death.* My present aim is to direct attention to a work of Heine's prime—not one of his last and decadent period.

As far back as 1837 the poet refers to this work in a letter to his publisher, Julius Campe. "I am busy day and night," he writes, "with my great book, the romance of my life, and now for

* *Vide* Heinrich Heine's Memoirs, edited by Gustav Karpeles: English version, John Lane, Publisher.

the first time I feel the full value of the papers that were lost in the fire at my mother's house. I had intended to publish this book later, but . . . it is to be the next book given to the public. You know I am no braggart, and I prophesy the most extraordinary results."

A few months later, writing to his Uncle Salomon Heine (with whom he was then in uncertain relations) the poet thus alludes to the work: "I have taken care that when we are all in our graves my whole life shall be known for what it has been."

The book so portentously referred to was long a subject of apprehension to Heine's wealthy relatives in Hamburg, to whom he was something of an *enfant terrible* and by whom his literary genius was held in small esteem; and the poet's occasional hint at publication may have been intended to keep them in proper disposition toward himself. I do not like to believe that he deliberately used it *in terrorem,* at least until the break that followed Uncle Salomon's death. It should be added, however, that there were many other persons outside the intimate Hamburg circle who heard with quakings of the spirit any rumor as to the threatened publication.

In 1839 Heine writes to Campe that he has

decided to postpone the bringing out of his Memoirs; but in 1840 writing to the same he admits having used a part of the work on Börne (a rather inferior production for Heine, in spite of some brilliant pages, and disfigured by personal malice; it was later in great part suppressed).

In 1840 we get a significant and meditated statement as to the Memoirs in a letter to Campe, as follows:

"I am quite happy and calm inwardly. I am used to abuse, and I know that the future is mine. Even if I were to die to-day, there remain four volumes of the story of my life, my Memoirs, which show forth all my thoughts and endeavors, and if only for their historical matter, for their true exposition of the most mysterious of transitive periods, will go down to posterity. The new generation will want to see the swaddling clothes that were its first covering."

This seems to indicate that Heine had finally resolved upon a posthumous publication of the book.

In 1845 the bitter dispute with his cousin, Karl Heine, relative to a financial provision for the poet (Uncle Salomon was now dead) broke out, and besides causing Heine great anguish of mind, hastened his end by the reaction upon his physical state. Writing to J. H. Detwold, Heine mentions a first offer of compromise by Karl, the condition being that he submit the MS. of the Memoirs to be "supervised" at Hamburg.

He writes to Campe (October, 1845):

"I am still in a most unpleasant position as regards my cousin, Karl Heine, for I do not agree with the form of payment. I will not agree to conditions—I will not forego the least particle of my dignity as an author or of the freedom of my pen, even if as a man I allow myself to be subjected to family considerations."

A few months later he informs Campe that he had tried the way of kindness pointed out to him by friends and by his own heart, in order to arrive at a settlement with his cousin; while the latter persisted in his injustice. Heine adds these memorable words:

"I have followed my softer feelings, while the cold voice of experience hissed in my ears that rarely is anything won from the hard men of money by tears and supplications in this world, but only by the sword. *My sword is my pen!*"

In the same letter, he says: "Yes, I have been working for some days at a horrible memoir in which the insolence of Karl Heine is shown up.

I shall drop my action, so that it may be seen that it is no longer a question of money. . . . I am calm, for I have done everything that a man can do for love (of his wife) and more."

Again he wrote to the same (1845):

"As for the undertaking which I am prepared to sign, it does not matter much how binding you make it. *I shall never, at any price, deliver up anything that I write to the censorship of my relations.*"

In this final step of the negotiations between the poet and his family, it is significant that not a word is said as to the destruction of any *existing manuscript* memoirs.

The upshot of the inheritance-quarrel was that Heine obtained a satisfactory settlement both for himself and, following his decease, for his wife Mathilde. On the other hand, though he is reticent as to the point, it seems probable that he complied with certain of Karl's wishes respecting the Memoirs.

What these wishes were, or what the conditions of the agreement reached by the poet and his kinsman, is not precisely known. But after Heine's death the manuscript fell into the hands of Uncle Salomon's family, who made such disposition of it as they saw fit. It is known that for many years past the papers have been sealed up in the archives of the Imperial Library at Vienna. Nor has official reserve ever suffered a hint to escape as to when, if ever, publication will be permitted.

William Sharp in his Life of Heine alludes to certain Memoirs "which the poet tells us that he himself destroyed". Evidently Mr. Sharp is here at fault, and most likely his reference is meant to cover "the papers that were lost in the fire at my mother's house",—as quoted above from Heine's letter (1837) to his publisher, Julius Campe.

That Heine expected his Memoirs would be published after his death and counted upon it to the very end, is placed beyond doubt by a piece of strong evidence. I allude to the incident related by Camille Selden, in her little book of reminiscences of Heine, entitled "The Last Days". "Camille Selden" was the pen-name used by a young German lady not otherwise clearly identified, who acted as reader for the poet in the last stage of his illness. She is said to have been a person of culture, charm and beauty, as beseemed the "Mouche" of the latest poems, and the poet seems to have felt a remarkable tenderness for her. Lovers of literature must always be grateful to this Unknown for giving the poet his last romance and his latest inspiration.

Camille Selden, then, relates how she entered Heine's room one day early in that fatal February, 1856, after he had undergone a dreadful attack of his disease, affecting both mind and body, and found him scribbling furiously on large sheets of paper with a pencil that seemed to her sharp as a deadly weapon. She continues:

"I heard a cruel laugh—the laugh of satiated revenge. I looked at Henri: 'I have them,' he cried, 'dead or living, they shall not escape. The tiger's claws shall survive the tiger.'"

Heine thus referred to his Memoirs, on which he had been even then working; and the story, though a shade melodramatic, may be accepted as true. There is no lack of testimony that he attached great importance to this "book of his life", as he called it. Most significant witness is offered by Alfred Meissner, to whom Heine once showed a box of MSS., remarking: "Look you! There are my memoirs. Therein I have been collecting for many years a series of portraits and frightful silhouettes. Many know of this box and tremble. In it is shut up one of my best, but by no means the last, of my triumphs."

SUCH is the unsatisfactory tale of Heine's personal memoirs, which the connoisseurs of literary scandal value at a higher rate than the lost "Confessions" of Byron. There can be little doubt that the matter of these unpublished manuscripts is worthy of Heine's fame, for the writing was begun when his powers were at the full. And as he scarcely ever wrote anything without literary value, even in his character of the modern Aretino, the harsh and long continued interdict on his own life-story must be resented by every lover of literature. It is some comfort, at least, that the work in all probability has not been destroyed, even though the sphinxes of authority remain mute, and say not when the ban will be removed and the precious pages given to the world. Lovers of Heine have only to console themselves with a reflection furnished by the Poet himself:

"To wait calmly is no loss of time for men to whom the future belongs."

Perhaps the world that is concerned with literature will not have much longer to wait for this particular gratification. It would not be surprising if, as a minor result of the Great War which has made such havoc with imperialisms, royal prescriptions and established orders in

Central Europe, the long-lost Memoirs of Heinrich Heine, hater of kings and despotisms, soldier of the liberation-war of humanity, were to
be recovered and made public by the decree of
a freed people. Nor can we doubt that the spirit
of Heine will smile approvingly upon this act of
tardy justice to his memory, which shall coincide
ironically with what he once predicted as the
"emancipation of kings"!

XI

THE IMMORALITY LEGEND

THE terrible disease from which Heine suffered a veritable crucifixion and which claimed in him its most illustrious victim, has entailed upon the poet some gratuitous moral censures. It was long hinted that his malady was but the natural result of an extreme libertinism, while pious persons viewed it as a special Divine chastisement for his sins. Legends imputing to him the most unheard-of sensuality and the most degrading vices were diligently propagated and are not yet extinct. I need not remind the observant reader that there is always a large class of people who are more interested in the alleged blackguardism of a poet than in his finest literary work. We see how the foul legend of Oscar Wilde's perversion is still kept alive and actively worked by not a few industrious writers for their profit. And you will note that both the literary concoctors of the Wilde legend and the public that greedily devour it are alike incapable of estimating the distinction of Wilde the artist.

An unfortunate and but too famous passage in one of Heine's later writings has given some color, in the minds of ill-judging persons, to the charges and suspicions above alluded to. It is quoted by Théophile Gautier as follows:

"I myself was the living law of morals, I was impeccable, I was purity incarnate; the most compromised of Magdalens were purified by the flames of my ardor and became virgins in my arms. These restorations to virginity went wellnigh at times, it is true, towards exhausting my holy strength. I was all love and wholly exempt from hatred. . . . Neither did I, as regards myself, acknowledge any friends, but many faithful believers, and I did them much good. The expenses attached to being a God, who can not be niggardly and who controls neither his purse nor his body, are enormous. In order to fulfil this splendid profession, one must above all things be dowered with much money and much health. Now one fine morning—it was toward the end of February, 1848—these two things failed me, and my divinity was so shaken that it fell miserably to pieces."

This fine piece of rhetoric—this purple patch of ironic exaggeration—has been worth to Heine a heavier sentence than its bad taste warranted. In a word, it has been taken as literally true, and it has offered a convenient foundation for the legend of Heine's "strange sins". The success of such slanders is due to the fact that they are equally relished by the pietistic, the prurient, and the frankly depraved.

And there is no basis in truth for the atrocious legend!

Heine never was a libertine, in the gross sense of the word, but it need not be denied that from early youth he was attractive to women, on account of his good looks, personal charm, and poetic fame.

There is no necessary relation between this fact of his agreeableness to women and consumption of the spinal marrow.

The poet was forced at one time to answer the calumnies that were being spread to account for his sickness, and he most solemnly denied that he had ever known the sort of "love" that is purchased. Even in verse he protests against the character of a *Don Juan* which his enemies were seeking to fasten upon him—and these lines are among the latest that he penned:

No maiden have I e'er misled
By tender words and flattering speech;
And if I knew a woman wed,
I counted her beyond my reach.

Were it not so, this name of mine
Would not deserve, forever writ
In honor's book to blaze and shine,
And in my face all men might spit!

This legend of libertinism as applied to Heine
limps very badly.

He met Mathilde in his 34th or 35th year,
loved her at once, and as we have seen, always
tenderly cherished her. Moreover, their love
was an incredibly ardent and tender passion (as
he tells his brother) and it lasted until the break-
down of his health. I believe his fidelity to
Mathilde is as well attested as his authorship of
the "Romancero".

There is another extremely important consid-
eration, always ignored by persons who do not
work with their brains, or who have no brains
to work with, viz.—

Heine was a constant producer of literature of
the first-class or of journalism that required very
uncommon abilities and close application. These

ambitions do not sort with the character of a careless libertine—a freebooter of the flesh, or a waster of time and health.

His letters, the witnesses of his private life, his delicate health from youth up, his known domestic character, are all opposed to the libertine theory. Hated as he was by enemies whose espionage never slept and scrupled at nothing, we should have had gross evidence of his immoralities if any such could have been obtained.

I can not find the note of the sensualist in his private letters or his literary productions. It is true he claimed the fullest artistic freedom, and he may be reproached with having gone beyond due bounds in a few instances. But this is not to convict him as a libertine, or we should make a pretty business of literary history!

The disease which killed him presented some exceptional features in his case, but generally speaking, it is the same which, in varying phases and manifestations, always threatens the sensitive, highly organized type of intellectual worker. Heine had prognostics of it from his twentieth year in the form of terrible headaches; "work and worry" easily and conclusively enough account for the worst that happened to him.

This fatality of the nervous organization is always taking its toll of victims: Daudet and Maupassant are among the more conspicuous examples of our time.

A candid and intelligent reading of the facts of Heine's life must acquit the poet of the heinous libel that has been brought against him in the name of morality.

XII

GOETHE AND HEINE

THE Juden-Schmerz of Heine, his Israel-sorrow, is often to be felt deep down under his manifold culture, his intellectualism, the irony he wears to protect his heart, and his Voltairian pose. He is the one Jew that has reached the first rank in literature, so the critics allow, and surely his is the most haunting lyric voice in modern letters. In his favor someone has significantly altered Browning's famous lines to make them read—

"O lyric voice, half *demon* and half bird,
And all a wonder and a wild desire!"

It was, of course, an English person who thus paraphrased—the English are nothing without their moral judgments, and Heine has given them surpassing provocation. Even Matthew Arnold, in his egregiously over-praised poem on

"Heine's Grave"—a disjointed prose homily for the most part, it seems to me—does not fail to rebuke him for his want of "love", leaning upon an alleged and somewhat doubtful censure of Goethe's. I wonder what Heine would have thought of the excellent Matthew Arnold, in conventional white choker and mutton-chop whiskers—an appalling figure of Anglican respectability—making him this preachment in Montmartre? And especially it would be worth while to get the poet's idea of the queer canting Arnoldian doxology:

> O thou, one of whose moods,
> Bitter and strange, was the life
> Of Heine—his strange, alas!
> His bitter life;—may a life
> Other and milder be mine!
> Mayst thou a mood more serene,
> Happier, have uttered in mine!

This comfortable aspiration of Matthew's, so eminently moral and, as it were, soothing and self-congratulatory—above all, so eminently English—would have delighted the ironic poet, however he might have viewed the rest of the sermon.

That dubious allusion of Goethe's, denying love to Heine, has long passed current for a profound reading of our poet's nature. I do not accept it as such, and I wonder that even Goethe's great name could have authorized the shallow misjudgment. It is worse—a malignant slander and a cunning defamation which would rob the poet of his divinest title. Love was not wanting to Heine; he possessed it in fullest measure and still inspires it in his world-wide audience, spite of the Gentile prejudice which is loth to recognize love or lovableness in a Jew. Hypocritical charity for his enemies he had none, and he neither asked nor gave quarter in his many battles. Yet he tells us: "I confess that I have scratched and bitten, and have been not exactly a lamb. But, believe me, those highly esteemed lambs of meekness would comport themselves less piously were they armed with the teeth and claws of the tiger. I can boast that I have only rarely made use of these actual weapons."

So the moralists have missed again, as they always do in dealing with a divinely enigmatic character like that of our poet. And finally without love Heine could not have had the Juden-Schmerz (for what is sorrow that knows not love?) which he has expressed for us in

verses that are vocal with lamentation and seem
to breathe the immemorial grief of Israel.

BREAK out in loud bemoaning,
My bitter martyr song,
That with never sigh nor groaning,
My heart has borne so long.

Go touch my hearers, wake them
To all that I have borne;
Go pierce their hearts and make them
Mourn as so long I mourn.

They weep, both great and humble,
The cold lords weep as well;
And women and flowers are weeping,
And tears in the stars do dwell.

And all these tears are going,
Together toward the South;
They go in one great flowing
To feed the Jordan's drouth.

Heine's description of his visit to Goethe, during the vacation in which he gathered materials
for his "Harz-Reise", is too well known to need
quotation here. The "plums that were looking

beautiful on the road to Weimar," is one of the
earliest and happiest phrases which the poet's
wit has made classic.   It is astonishing, by the
way, how many such shibboleths we owe to that
fertile, epigrammatic genius.

In a letter to his friend Moser, dated Göttingen, July, 1825, Heine thus measures himself
with Goethe—an immense piece of presumption
in the young man, and yet at the same time a
remarkable proof of his self-knowledge.   The
letter runs in part:

"Goethe and I are fundamentally of such a
nature that from our very heterogeneity we must
repel each other.   He is essentially an easy-living
man for whom the joy of life is the highest, one
who feels life for and in the idea of it, has a sort
of foreshadowing of it and expresses it in poems,
but has never laid a firm hand on it, and still less
has lived it.   I, on the other hand, am essentially
an enthusiast; that is, one who is inspired with
an idea, even to the point of sacrifice, and I am
always forced to lose myself in it.   But, on the
other hand, I have seized firmly the joy of life
and the delight of it, and now there is in me the
great struggle between my clear reason, which
sanctions the joy of living, and denies all sacrifices in inspiration or folly, and my enthusiastic

tendency which often leaps up in me, inundates and takes possession of me, and perhaps drags me *down* again to its ancient realm, though it is, perhaps, better to say, draws *up;* for it is still a great question, whether the enthusiast, who gives even his life for his idea, does not live more, and more happily than Herr von Goethe in all his six and seventy years of egoism and comfort."

There was one point, however, in regard to Goethe upon which Heine never wavered or weakened, *i. e.,* his loyal admiration for the greatest of German poets. Goethe's work inspired some of his most brilliant pages, beginning in youth with the "Pictures of travel" and ending in his latter years with that quaint conceit, "Doctor Faust", intended for dramatic representation, and which will always be prized for its wonderful preface, in which he summarizes the Faust legends.

XIII

BIMINI

IT has been said—doubtless by some Christian critic who was in no hurry to leave this cold world for Abraham's warm bosom—that Heine "loved life too much", and a sick-bed remark of his is quoted, that he would gladly change his lot to be a poodle joyously frisking in the sunshine on the pavement below his window.

It is at any rate true that he loved life intensely, from his great humanness, as I see it, which critics have been little in the habit of remarking, but which seems to me one of the deepest traits of the poet. In spite of his terrible disorder, which almost completely annulled his sensory powers, Heine to the very end continued to "savor" the good earth, and to feel a profound attachment to the homely things of life.

The chords slip from my feeble hand, the glass
  Breaks into atoms, which with heart aglow,
    A moment since to merry lips I prest.

177

O God! how bitter 'tis to die, to pass!
  O God! how sweet it is to live below
    Here, in the old, familiar earthly nest!

Heine's unquenchable longing for life under
the Destroyer's hand* is most quaintly and touchingly expressed in the last—perhaps the greatest
—of his poems, which describes an imaginary
voyage to the fabled Isle of Bimini and the
magic fountain of Ponce de Leon:

  Who discovered Florida,
  But for many a year long, vainly
  Wandering, sought the wondrous island
  His soul yearned for—Bimini!

The poem is a long one for Heine, but not a
line could be spared; and all the old magic in-
gredients are to be found in it, including his
irony, active to the last. As a whole this poem is
a wonderful piece of genius and true imagination: the production of a man more than half
dead, it must be regarded as a "triumph of mind

* In 1848—eight years before the end—Heine writes to
Julius Campe:
"My mind is free and clear, and even cheerful. My heart
is sound, almost sound enough to be eager for and *greedy of
life*—and my body is so paralyzed, so rotten!"

over matter". Let us briefly trace this last vision
of the stricken dreamer.

> BIMINI! at the enchanting
> Sound of thy sweet name, my bosom
> Heaves, and the forgotten visions
> Of my perished youth return;
>
> Faded garlands deck their foreheads,
> Woefully their glances greet me,
> And dead nightingales pipe faintly
> A slow dying melody.
>
> Startled, I spring up and trembling
> So thro' all this wasted body
> That the seams of my fool's jacket
> Burst asunder. Ah, but I
>
> Needs must laugh the moment after,
> For methinks I hear the babble
> Of droll melancholy parrots
> Babbling round me, "Bimini!"

In all of Heine there is nothing more grimly
ironic than the last verse—but this time a strain
of self-pity qualifies the bitterness of the ever
recurring mood. And the poet seems to be al-

lured in spite of himself. Lovely visions of the wondrous Isle throng upon the sick man's fancy, and he becomes almost credulous of the ancient legend. Ah, Heaven! if it might be true.

> In the Isle of Bimini
> Blooms the everlasting Spring-time;
> Golden larks in azure heavens
> Warble sweet their tirili.

> Lissome wild flowers over-wander
> Lustrous meadows, rich savannahs
> Glowing with voluptuous colors,
> Breathing passionatest odors.

> Lofty palms above them waving,
> Ever tremulously tranquil,
> To the flow'rets underneath them
> Waft fresh kisses of cool shadow.

> In the Isle of Bimini
> Springs the all-delightful Fountain,
> And from that dear fountain ever
> Flows the youth-restoring water.

Ho! then for Bimini and its water of life. Who will sail with the poet on his barque builded

of stout trochees, with Fancy at the prow, a
breeze of Good Humor in the sails, and Wit for
ship-mate (long have they been of Skipper Heinrich's crew!)? Noble lords, have you any gouty
twinges?—fair ladies, have you spied any lurk-
ing wrinkles in your beauty?—

> Follow me to Bimini,
> There shall you be surely rid of
> All such troublesome discomforts—
> Hydropathic is the cure.

Our ship is bravely equipped, and our colors—

> Black, Red, Gold—romantic colors!
> Tricolor of Barbarossa,
> Which I've also seen at Frankfort,
> In the town church of St. Paul's.

But ere we set sail on the wondrous voyage,
the human heart of the poet gives a tender
thought to the familiar presences, the humble
friends of hearth and home.

> To that land of youth eternal
> To the Isle of Bimini
> Yearns my spirit, yearn my senses:
> Fare you well, beloved companions!

Thou old house-cat, Mimili,
And old house-cock, Krikriki,
Fare ye well, we come not, we,
Back again from Bimini.

Alas! we come back but too soon, as wise and
as fortunate as the old hidalgo Ponce de Leon,
having like him reached the long-sought Isle of
Bimini—

The still land, wherein so softly,
Under silent cypress shadows,
Flows the streamlet whose good water
Likewise hath strange power to heal.

Lethe! that good water's name is—
Drink thereof, and thou forgettest
All thy suffering,—yea, forgotten
Thou and all thy suffering, too!

Heine drank the Lethean cup unshrinkingly
when it came to him, but he did not reach for it
an instant before the due time. Like the Sad-
ducee, he was sure only of this life, and bitter as
it had been made for him in his closing years,
he savored it to the last dregs. "Dying," he said,
"is something to shudder at, but not death, if
indeed death do exist. Perhaps it is the last
superstition!"

XIV

BODY AND SOUL

FROM the royal Hadrian's *Animula, vagula, blandula*, perhaps the most famous, in a literary sense, of all premortem utterances, to Heine's *Leib und Seele* ("Body and Soul") is a far step in point of time, and the contrast as regards the sentiment is likewise extraordinary.

The imperial Roman gives as it were the last sigh of Paganism—is there anything so hopeless and sad in remembered Latin literature as these few fluttering lines that have a certain wonderful likeness to the fading accents of life itself? Hadrian was not a great poet, and he belonged to the decadent age of Roman letters, but these few lines of his are both classic and immortal. And, strange to say, they have furnished inspiration (not always faithfully acknowledged) to many a Christian poet.*

* Very notably to Alexander Pope, whose beautiful verses, "The Dying Christian to His Soul", universally known to English readers, were confessedly suggested by Hadrian's lines.

Heine's poem anticipatory of his own death has two things in common with Hadrian's lines—the seal of originality and the stamp of a remarkable utterance. In addition, of course, it has both irony and humor, which in this connection the ancient world would not have understood at all, and which, in its peculiar Heinesque quintessence and combination, the modern world of letters has not yet, maybe, happily assimilated.

Hadrian and Heine! What an apt alliterative apposition and, at the same time, contrast the learned preceding critics and commentators have left me to discover! Nor is it a mere freak of fancy that couples these names otherwise so antipodal in association. Both have uttered a memorable farewell to life and so obtained the coveted prize of immortality for their words—equal guerdon to him of the purple and him of the lyric laurel.

But frankly, I prefer Heine's poem, and I do not believe the literature of the world has anything in kind to compare with it.

THE poor Soul speaketh to its Clay:
"I cannot leave thee thus; I'll stay
With thee, with thee in death I'll sink,
And black Annihilation drink!

Thou still hast been my second I,
Embracing me so lovingly,
A satin feast-robe round my form,
Doubled with ermine soft and warm.
Woe's me! I dare not face the fact—
Quite disembodied, quite abstract,
To loiter as a blessed Naught
Above there in the realms of Thought,
Through Heavenly Halls, immense and frigid,
Where the Immortal dumb and rigid
Yawn to me as they clatter by
With leaden clogs so wearily.
Oh, it is horrible! Oh, stay,
Stay with me, thou beloved Clay!"

The Body to the poor Soul said:
"Oh, murmur not, be comforted!
We all should quietly endure
The wounds of Fate, which none can cure.
I was the lamp's wick, and to dust
Consume; but thou, the Spirit, must
Be saved with care, and lifted far
To shine in Heaven, a little star
Of purest light. I am but cinder,
Mere matter, rubbish, rotten tinder,
Losing the shape we took at birth,
Mouldering again to earth in earth.

Now, fare thee well and grieve no more!
Perchance life is not such a bore
In Heaven, as you expect up there.
If you should meet the old Great Bear
(Not Meyer-Bear*) i' the starry climes,
Greet him from me a thousand times!"

    * A play upon the name of Meyerbeer, the great composer,
a personal friend of Heine's.

NOTE A

HEINE's exile entailed very real hardships and privations, whatever his enemies may have alleged to the contrary. The poet testifies:

"By a decree of the Government of my native country not only were all my previous writings prohibited, but also everything that I might write in the future. My brain was confiscated and my poor innocent stomach was by this interdict deprived of every means of sustenance. At the same time my name was to be erased from the memory of man, and all the censors of my native country received strict injunctions to strike out every passage in the newspapers, and in pamphlets and books in which I was mentioned, whether favorably or unfavorably. Shortsighted fools! These resolutions and injunctions were powerless against an author whose spiritual interests issued victorious from every persecution, even if his finances were brought to utter ruin, so that even now I can trace the effects of their paltry malice. But I did not starve, although at that time I was pressed hard enough by grim want. Living in Paris is so expensive, especially if a man is married and has no children, for these dear little dolls while away the time for the husband and wife, and they have no need to seek amusement away from home, where it costs so much. And then I never learned the art by which the hungry manage to live on mere words, the more so as nature has given me such a comfortable appearance that no one would believe in my necessity. The poverty-stricken fellows who have had help from me laughed when I told them that in future I would have to starve. Was I not related to all sorts of millionaires? Had not the generalissimo of millionaires, had not the millionairissimo* called me his friend—his friend? I could never convince my clients that the great millionairissimo called me his friend precisely because I did not ask money of him; had I done so, that would have been the end of his friendship!"

* This reference is undoubtedly to the Baron Rothschild of Paris, with whom Heine had a slight acquaintance. See Note C.

NOTE B

THE verses of which Gautier was reminded on seeing the large coffin and the shrunken form of the poet are given below. They are not of Heine's later work, as some commentators have mistakenly supposed, but belong to his youth and are touchingly related to his Amalie-sorrow.

MY songs, so old and bitter,
  My dreams, so vile and drear,
Come, bury them forever—
  What ho! a coffin here!

Much will I lay within it
  Which yet I may not tell:
The size of Heidelberg's famed tun
  That coffin must excel.

See that a bier be furnished
  Of stout and seasoned pine;
Let it be longer than the bridge
  At Mainz that spans the Rhine.

And summon me twelve giants,
  Men of a mightier mould
Than Christopher the Sainted
  In Köln's cathedral old.

Let these bear forth the coffin
  And drown it in the sea;
For to so great a coffin
  The grave as huge must be.

Wouldst know wherefore the coffin
  Must be so strong and vast?—
There all my love and anguish
  I'll lay to rest at last.

NOTE C

Of the excellent Baron James de Rothschild of Paris, head of the world-renowned financial house of that name in Heine's time (about 1841), the poet has made a most witty and inimitable satirical sketch. If one were ever tempted to think of Heine in Carlylean terms,* it is only necessary to recall this wonderful caricature of Rothschild:—no Jew (again in the Carlylean or discreditable reading) could have brought himself to do so much irreverence to money as personified in the great Banker.

But—and this is a convenient place to note it—Heine cared no more for money, in the worshipful sense, than did Baruch Spinoza, and, I suspect, even less than the average countryman of Tammas of Craigenputtock.

Heine's humor is a trifle over-ripe in parts of the skit, but the whole is so deeply stamped with what some have been pleased to call his diabolic quality, and is withal of such concentrated wit and wise malice, that it well deserves to be given *sans* expurgation. I content myself with slightly paraphrasing a Rabelaisian turn or two.

"On an occasion several years ago when I went to see Herr Rothschild, a liveried servant carried a certain utensil of private convenience to the great man across the corridor, and a speculator who happened to pass at the same moment

* Heine was one of Carlyle's "pet aversions", according to Frank Harris:—*vide* the latter's "Contemporary Portraits".

191

took off his hat reverently to the same. So far, I say it with all gravity, goes the respect of certain people. I made a note of the name of that devout man, and I am convinced that in time he will be a millionaire. Once when I told Herr —— that I had lunched *en famille* with Baron Rothschild in the chambers of his bank, he clapped his hands together in astonishment and told me that I had enjoyed an honor which has hitherto been granted only to those of Rothschild's blood or to certain reigning princes, an honor for which he would sell half his nose. I will say that the nose of Herr ——, even if it were shortened by half, would still be of a prodigious length.

"A superfluity of wealth is harder to bear than poverty. I advise any one who is in great need of money to go to Herr von Rothschild; not to borrow of him (for I doubt if he would get anything much), but to find solace by the sight of that moneyed misery. The poor devil who has too little and cannot help himself will be convinced that there is a man who is far more wretched, because he has too much money; because all the money has flowed into his cosmopolitan giant pocket, and he has to carry about with him such a burden, while round him the great horde of the hungry and the thieves hold out their hands towards him. And what terrible and dangerous hands they are! 'How are you?' a German poet once asked the Herr Baron. 'I am mad,' he answered. 'Until you throw money out of the window,' said the Poet, 'I won't believe it.' But the Baron said with a sigh, 'That is my madness, that I do *not* throw money out of the window.'

"How unhappy are the rich in this life; and after death they do not even go to Heaven! 'It is easier for a camel to pass through the eye of a needle than for a rich man to enter into the Kingdom of Heaven'—and that sentence of the Divine communist is a fearful anathema, and shows his bitter hatred of the *Bourse* and *haute finance* of Jerusalem."

NOTE D

HEINE bade farewell to Hamburg and Germany in this characteristic fashion:

> GIVE me a wide and noble field,
> Where there at least is room to die!
> O from this narrow huckstering world,
> Ere I am stifled, let me fly!
>
> Their meat and drink is of the best,
> And, blind as moles, they take their pleasure;
> The opening in a poor-box lid
> Their charity would more than measure.
>
> Cigar in mouth, and idle hands
> Stuck in their pockets, see them pass!
> Their stomachs are beyond reproach—
> 'Tis how to stomach *them,* alas!
>
> They deal in every spice that grows,
> But roots, the sweetest, cannot quell
> The putrid foulness of their souls
> That vile as rotten haddocks smell.
>
> O had I seen some monstrous vice,
> Some crime colossal, bloody, found—
> Aught save these virtues, morals smug
> Of twenty shillings in the pound!

Ye clouds above, O bear me forth
To Africa, to Lapland drear:
To Pomerania itself—
No matter where, if far from here!

O take me with you! But the clouds
Are far too wise to pause or heed.
For, when they travel o'er this town,
They hurry on at double speed.

NOTE E

THE tedium of that living death could only be described by the sufferer himself (his agony lasted so long that, as Gautier observed, he was forgotten of the world), and indeed he has done it with a fearful imaginative power in these verses, which were among the last from his pen:

> How wearily time crawls along,
> That hideous snail that hastens not,
> While I, without the power to move,
> Am ever fixed to one dull spot.
>
> Upon my dreary chamber wall
> No gleam of sunshine can I trace;
> I know that only for the grave,
> Shall I exchange this hopeless place.
>
> Perhaps already I am dead,
> And these maybe are phantoms vain;
> These motley phantasies that pass
> At night through my disordered brain.
>
> Perhaps with ancient heathen shapes,
> Old faded gods, this brain is full,
> Who for their most unholy rites,
> Have chosen a dead poet's skull;

And charming frightful orgies hold,
The madcap phantoms!—all the night,
That in the morning this dead hand
About their revelries may write.

TRANSLATIONS

I HAVE throughout this book quoted liberally from an American edition of Heine's complete works, of which the translation was made by the late Charles Godfrey Leland. This translation is, upon the whole, a good one, though often lacking smoothness and verbal felicity. It could be improved undoubtedly by omitting some of the translator's notes. Indeed I regard many of Leland's glosses upon his author as in very questionable taste. Leland as a commentator is frequently irritating, often absurd, and sometimes preposterous. His awkwardly ambitious attempt to supply a corrective to what he conceives to have been Heine's frequent lapses from good judgment and taste, as well as the poet's alleged occasional defects of literary form, is the one thing that can fairly be urged against this generally competent edition. The translator's lack of wit, by comparison with his original, is painfully evident—and herein Heine has his due revenge.

With this reservation, it must be said that one or two of Leland's prefaces, with a large part of his annotations and footnote commentaries, are of high value. The translator was himself a ripe and versatile scholar, with a full share of the professed scholar's pedantry and egotism. It is a pity that as a literary politician and casuist he deemed himself competent to play the censor toward a far greater man and writer,—and succeeded only in making himself a bore of the first magnitude. Leland was amusingly anxious to be thought a cosmopolite (as attested by many of his interjected commentaries), but the native "freshness" of the American is written all over his "editing" of Heine.

I have not, however, strictly limited myself to the Leland prose translation; as for the poetical selections, I have generally preferred the renderings of Mr. Gilbert Cannan, one of the latest and most gifted of Heine's interpreters.

The French translations of Heine's prose undoubtedly take the palm and may be read with the pleasure of a new work when one is already familiar with the original or with English versions. Many of the poems have been exquisitely rendered into French prose, and in this work the hand of Gérard de Nerval may be identified (to whom Heine himself gives eloquent praise). But as might be expected, the French have not succeeded so well in the metrical translations: here the kinship of our language to the German has given the English translators a decided superiority.